Promises

THE LIFE AND LOVE OF AN
AMERICAN BORN IN NORTH KOREA

JOON BAI

TRANS WESTERN PICTURES, LLC | PLEASANTON, CA

Published by
Trans Western Pictures, LLC | Pleasanton, CA

    Publisher's Cataloging-in-Publication Data
    Bai, Joon.

    Promises : the life and love of an American born in
    North Korea / Joon Bai. – Pleasanton, CA : Trans Western
    Pictures, LLC, 2022.

    p. ; cm.

    ISBN13: 978-0-9601151-0-5

    1. Bai, Joon. 2. Korean Americans--Biography.
    2. Screenwriters--United States--Biography. I. Title.

    E184.K6 B35 2022
    973.04957--dc23

Project coordination by Jenkins Group, Inc. | www.jenkinsgroupinc.com

Interior design by Brooke Camfield

Printed in Korea
26   25   24   23   22 • 5   4   3   2   1

To my Kyuhee, for her endearing love for me.
Love is God's gift.
It is the most magnificent, splendorous thing,
an affair that will last for eternity.

Contents

Introduction

I once wrote a screenplay for a movie, *The Other Side of the Mountain.*

I began writing it while I was traveling to North Korea to help offer humanitarian aid for North Korean orphanages and farmers when the country was devastated by a severe famine from 1996 to 1998.

I was inspired by actual events I had experienced during the Korean War, when I was a young boy, when my family and I made an arduous and painful journey south in 1950 as refugees, part of a vast human tragedy.

What had motivated and inspired me to begin writing? Who encouraged me? Why?

The story of my life and the answers unfold in *Promises.*

The Other Side of the Mountain is the only film I wrote and produced. It was the first feature film co-produced between an American and the Democratic People's Republic of Korea.

The Other Side of the Mountain took six years to complete under extremely difficult circumstances that called for delicate negotiations that would in the end prove fruitful. I was able to win the consent of the Department of Culture of the North Korean government to produce the film with North Koreans. The film was shot entirely on location in North Korea, and the cast and crew were North Koreans who received rations from the government for working on the movie, like any other job. For an American, such permission was unprecedented.

In my screenplay, I told the story of two young lovers brought together then wrenchingly forced apart by the Korean War. The efforts of the lovers to reunite were poignant, made more difficult by the formidable demarcation line along the 38th parallel that had cleaved the country into two separate lands and is still in place today.

My screenplay, and ultimately the movie itself, is a cry for Korea's unification, told through the voices of North Koreans.

I wanted to tell the story that showed that the forced separation of loved ones is among the most painful of human experiences.

While we were making the film, I observed what the poor conditions and lack of infrastructure in North Korea had done to its people. I learned also that ordinary citizens acting as extras had a deep desire to express their dreams and hopes for peace and reunification.

That is the indelible force that brought us together and allowed us to create *The Other Side of the Mountain*.

The Other Side of the Mountain touched a chord with viewers worldwide. I would receive enthusiastic responses from viewers of all ages in both North and South Korea, as well as rave reviews and awards at more than twenty film festivals around the world, and later showings on Amazon, Netflix, and YouTube. The viewers would say time and again that *The Other Side of the Mountain*'s tragic love story, beautiful cinematography, stirring soundtrack, and moving performances had touched them deeply.

"Joon, God created you to make this film, and you did it," my beloved wife, Kyuhee, had told me.

My many friends and business associates later asked me to make a documentary of the making of *The Other Side of the Mountain*. Some said I should write a book. I accepted the challenge.

When I began to write the script for the documentary, I tapped memories of my eventful life, growing up in North Korea in idyllic days before World War II and later more tumultuous times during that war and the Korean War. I also thought back to my challenging and fruitful years of coming to America for the education that set me on a path to great success and sparked my successful business and my yearning to offer humanitarian aid to the people of North Korea.

That in turn led me to write the story of my life you now hold in your hands. I wanted to write about my mother's shining love for me and of my splendid love affair with Kyuhee.

Looking back at all my many achievements, sacrifices, and devotions, I learned that there is nothing more glorious than loving someone.

Kyuhee was the greatest gift God gave to me.

CHAPTER ONE

A Love Story

I have a date every Sunday with my beloved wife, Kyuhee. We have been together for nearly sixty years.

This Sunday, February 14, 2021, was Kyuhee's birthday and Valentine's Day. This morning I made breakfast for Kyuhee, hard-boiled egg, an English muffin with butter and grape jelly, a slice of crispy bacon, and a thin wedge of watermelon. I had the same.

Then I packed a cooler with a bottle of chardonnay and a turkey sandwich, grabbed bouquets of orchids, her favorite flowers, and roses, and set out for a ride to the memorial park. The day was bright, the sky blue, the air fresh, and the sound of music in the car set a pleasant mood.

We both love opera, and I selected two of Kyuhee's favorite arias, "Vissi de'arte" from Puccini's *Tosca* and "Un bel di vedremo" from his other masterwork, *Madame Butterfly*. They are sad laments of lost love. "Vissi de'arte's" lyrics remind me of Kyuhee:

I lived for love
I never did harm to a living soul
With a secret hand, I relieved as many misfortunes as I knew
Always with true faith, I gave flowers to the altar

The arias expressed Kyuhee's compassion for her fellow human beings and her deep faith in God. She cried when she heard these arias at the opera.

For a change of pace, I played Dean Martin's "I Have but One Heart." I like his cool, laid-back style and crooning voice. My selection best captured the love I have for Kyuhee.

> *I have but one heart, this heart I bring to you*
> *I have but one dream that I can cling to*
> *You are the one dream I pray comes true*
> *You are my one love in my life, and I live for you*

As I came near the park, I called out, "Kyuhee, I am coming."

My Kyuhee passed away on October 26, 2019, at 7:26 a.m. I held her hand and watched her breathe her last breath. She died peacefully in my arms and was with God.

She now lies at the Oakmont Memorial Park and Mortuary overlooking a spectacular view of nearby Mount Diablo and Briones Regional Park near our Pleasanton, California, home. As John Steinbeck described it in *East of Eden*, the park is green in the winter but golden brown in the summer. I felt a gentle, cool breeze touch my face. The black marble headstone is etched at the top with our last name: BAI. On the right-hand side, it reads:

> *Kyuhee*
> *February 14, 1935–October 26, 2019*
> *In memory of the most beautiful mother and wife*
> *who endeared herself to all of us with her love and grace*

On the left-hand side is my name, Joon, and my birth date: September 3, 1937, with a space for our reunion date.

Lilacs and begonias, scented and beautiful, sit on each side of the stone in the brisk morning air, and two marble benches sit in front. In the middle of the headstone is a heart-shaped photograph of us.

I stood with one hand touching the stone and thanked God for this beautiful day. As always, I kissed Kyuhee and greeted her.

"I missed you. James and Stephen and our grandsons are doing well, and I got a second Covid vaccine this morning, and I am feeling fine."

I then replaced the flowers in the vases with my Valentine roses, watered the plants, and sat on the bench. I opened the bottle of chardonnay and told Kyuhee about the past week's events. I fell into the memories of our travel together and shared with her one story.

"Do you remember our first trip to Europe, Vienna, a city of confection? The concierge at the reception desk gave us two canceled tickets for *Madame Butterfly* at the Vienna Opera. At the end of the opera, I saw you in tears, and you said how wonderful they performed, and how sad you felt for the Cho-Cho-san, remember?"

I took a sip of chardonnay.

I opened a letter Kyuhee wrote to me in 1963, when I was studying in Columbia, Missouri, and she stayed in Chicago to continue her nursing job at Wesley Memorial.

Dear Joon:
I wish to thank you for the card you sent for my birthday.

I placed it next to our picture on the desk.

You expressed in the card how deeply you love me.

I always wished to say to you the priceless gift God gave me was you.

I *promise* to you that I will devote the fullest to you and love you until my last breath.

I believe God gave us this time of our separation, so we feel the depth and width of our love for each other.

I will hold a bundle of our love gingerly and not be hurt forever.

I love you,
Kyuhee

I opened the card she wrote in 1984 when we moved to Danville, California.

Dear Joon:
I thank God for his *promises* of the blessing of our love and the move to Northern California. I adore being your wife because it is a joy and challenge.

I admire your courage and willingness to tackle the unknown.

In your life, it is an adventure I genuinely enjoy riding with you.

Happy 19th anniversary!!

I love you,
Kyuhee

Kyuhee showed me her love every minute of our lives together. Kyuhee brought out the best in me. She encouraged me to succeed in business, help North Koreans in desperate need unconditionally, and create the award-winning movie *The Other Side of the Mountain*.

Meeting Kyuhee was the most glorious event in my life.

CHAPTER TWO

My Early Years

My name is Bai Byung Joon. I was born in 1937 in Haeryong, Ham Kyung Book-Do, Korea, in what is now the Democratic People's Republic of Korea, more familiarly known as North Korea.

Haeryong was a city of one hundred thousand nestled in lush highlands on the banks of the Tumen River, which serves as the border between China, North Korea, and Russia.

I was the third son of six children, four brothers and two sisters. My early childhood was peaceful, filled with love, playing with my siblings, and learning at school.

That peace would be shattered when my family was swept into the savagery and destruction of war caused by Japan's imperial aggression as the second Sino-Japanese war intensified. The Japanese made it a mission to erase Korean culture, language, and history by forcing the school system to assimilate Koreans into Japanese ways.

They took properties from ordinary citizens, tarnished a five-thousand-year-old culture, and undermined the gentle philosophies of simple farmers in their white-colored garments. They replaced our name with a Japanese name and slashed Koreans' pride and dignity with their samurai swords.

Japanese turned the "Land of Morning Calm" into a gateway to conquer China, and eventually, other East and Southeast Asian countries.

My grandfather, Bai Hyung Gi, died from a heart attack at forty-four. His younger brother Bai Jung Gi took my father and his three sisters as his own. Growing up, we looked to Jung Gi as our grandfather.

He was a wealthy man, the most affluent in Ham Kyung Book-Do province. He owned thousands of hectares of land, and his company produced lumber products, harvested high on local mountains thick with trees.

His workers would cut trees then float them down the Tumen River to a bend near Haeryong. There, the logs were chained and pulled into the mill, and electric motor-driven saws cut them into railroad ties for the expanding rail system being built by Korean laborers under the direction of the Japanese colonial government.

My grandfather was an adventurous person and an astute businessman, and he would run his business smoothly throughout the years of Japanese colonization.

My father ran the factory operations for my grandfather after graduating from Kyoto University in Japan. He was handsome, keen-minded, intelligent, and had a preternatural way of charming townspeople, and they liked him. Like his father, he was a prominent figure in our community.

∽

My father provided accommodations in our estate's guesthouse for Japanese General Hida, the commanding officer of an army transportation regiment stationed in Haeryong. The general and his wife had two daughters, a six-year-old named Akiko, my age, and an infant. The general's wife could not produce enough milk for her baby. My mother, still nursing my younger brother Ken, fed both infants.

Akiko's mother often brought a box of rice cakes, beautifully wrapped, to my mother to show her appreciation.

Akiko, a pretty and joyful girl, became my only friend, and we spent most of our days playing with her toys. I remember Akiko serving me apple juice and rice cakes, just as her mother served tea to the general. I learned how to speak Japanese from Akiko and Maru, her maid.

My mother often gathered her sons in our backyard and taught us to write Korean. First, she would write the Hangul (alphabet), using a bamboo stick to draw consonants and vowels in the sandbox we often played in.

General Hida would at times invite other generals to his house, our estate guesthouse. I remember their thin mustaches and how they would drink and sing. One evening, curious about the swords they wore as part of their uniforms, I walked to the guesthouse where visiting generals had placed them on a bench. I touched one of the different, ornate hilts of the swords. I pulled one from its hilt and barely touched the blade with my finger. I was shocked at its razor-sharpness and could easily have cut my finger.

ᔖ

Other than the general's occasional dinner gathering, there were no Japanese soldiers or military police presence on our estate at any time.

Japanese influence was pervasive. Haeryong served as a transportation center for troops and supplies as Japan continued its ill-fated efforts to take over China and Asia as World War II spread.

My hometown became a means to Japanese ends and existed to serve Japan, which is why it remained relatively calm. One day, my father told us that he heard from a friend in Beijing that the Japanese army had started to retreat from central China and was on the brink of defeat in the war. Life became more fraught. My peaceful childhood was ending.

Japanese soldiers led by local sympathizers searched the town to confiscate any item made from metal, mainly silver utensils. Father said that the Japanese military was running out of material to manufacture weapons, equipment, and ammunition.

A Japanese platoon ranged through town and shot and killed all the dogs running in the streets, which they said was the prelude to their passing through towns during their retreat.

One early morning, my mother told me Akiko and her family had left without saying farewell. I ran up to Akiko's room and found a note on top of a soft teddy bear, her favorite toy.

"Sayonara, Hey-Joon (my Japanese name). I will remember your dimple." She had left the teddy bear for me as a farewell gift.

That evening, I wondered why she had to go, and the thought of losing my friend and only playmate saddened me.

Everyone was talking about the war coming to an end.

Soon after, my brothers and I heard the crackle of gunshots and the sound of bombs exploding all around us. Through gaps in the wood panels shielding our windows, we watched the Japanese rushing to get out of town. Father said they were evacuating to nearby Rajin, a seaport where naval ships waited to transport them back to Japan.

What we saw next horrified us.

Japanese soldiers killed Koreans on the street indiscriminately, including older men, women, and children. It was an atrocious act.

Father told us Japanese soldiers were trying to kill members of the Korean Liberation Army who might be hiding in the crowd. He also said they fired at innocent Koreans to empty their ammunition and discard their weapons to lighten the loads they carried. After the Japanese soldiers had left, people emerged from hiding and began to carry the dead bodies from the street, wailing and banging the ground with their fists.

While all this was happening, we remained safe. Father thought that General Hida ordered the retreating Japanese armies not to harm our family.

༽

After the Japanese evacuation, followed by the defeat of the Japanese empire and the end of the Second World War, our country was liberated.

On August 15, 1945, it became an independent nation after thirty-six years of Japanese colonization. However, a new horror awaited us.

"White Russians," soldiers with pale, milky faces, blondish-white hair, and green-blue eyes surged into town without firing a single shot. They were armed with long, single-action rifles with bayonets affixed to what appeared to be ancient World War I rifles I had seen in a photograph.

Their faces were crusted with dirt, their uniforms were filthy, and they exuded an intensely pungent odor as if they had never bathed nor brushed their teeth in their lives. They slept on haystacks and laid their heads on loaves of hard, black bread as pillows.

They appeared to be primitive people who had lived in isolated places in the Russian Far East, far from civilization. They walked the streets in groups, constantly chewing and spitting sunflower seeds. They would approach people on the road without speaking, and pantomime smoking a cigarette, then simply take cigarettes from people's pockets without asking.

We called Russian soldiers "Russki." One day, three Russkies came to our house and chatted with my father, who spoke a few words of Russian. Then, my brothers and I saw them demanding cigarettes from my father. He gave them two packs. They split the packs, placed one cigarette behind each ear, and stashed the rest in their pockets.

After that day, my father and mother went to our farm to stay away from the Russkies and from young communist guerilla fighters searching for Japanese sympathizers. My father instructed two elderly couples who lived on the estate to take care of us and the two horses we kept.

Shortly after my parents left, four Russkies appeared at our door, pointing their rifles at my brothers and me and gesturing to us to step outside the house and stay away. Within minutes, we heard desperate, piercing cries.

One by one, they raped Sun Ja, our seventeen-year-old servant. She screamed in a high-pitched voice, "Save me, save me, mother, mother."

It seemed to us that an eternity had passed before the Russkies left. We rushed inside to find Sun Ja, shaking, crying, and burying her head in a blood-covered blanket.

"Do not touch me. Do not touch me," she repeated, sobbing.

After raping her, the soldiers had urinated on the floor surrounding Sun-Ja, soaking the blanket and her dress. She was severely hurt, bleeding, and shaking as she continued to cry for her mother. We could not comprehend such a barbaric act. We shouted, "Russkies are animals. Russkies are savages."

One of the elderly caretakers went to the farmhouse and informed Father about what had happened. Father and Mother came home and called a doctor to treat Sun Ja. Sun Ja was sick for a few days with a high fever. She did not speak for months.

My mother had raised Sun Ja after the influenza pandemic took her parents when she was very young. She had one distant uncle but no close relative. My brothers and I looked at her as our older sister. Everyone in our family felt hurt for her suffering for a long time.

の

After liberation from the Japanese, Korean guerrilla fighters, made up of young Marxist followers who fought against the Japanese in Manchuria, arrived in town searching for Japanese sympathizers, whom they called the "bourgeois."

With thin, dark faces and moving like Jodo tutors, they searched door-to-door on tips they received from their families and friends. They exposed their brutality by killing people they saw as Japanese sympathizers in the public park with their bare hands. Five or six young guerrilla fighters would stand in a circle flinging their victims, still alive, with extreme head-snapping precision as if practicing judo.

Eventually, after repeated crashes to the ground, the victims would lose consciousness and die on the dirt. The young guerrillas would simply walk away, leaving their victims on the ground. We did not see any blood. Such was the force of the horrible game that all died of internal bleeding.

Townspeople simply watched the entire event in spellbound horror. I thought Japanese imperialists created the time for Russians to rape us, forcing our brothers to murder each other and leaving thousands of mothers in tears.

Many South Koreans collaborated with the Japanese to torture and killed fellow brothers. "Where was a sense of humanity and conscience in those traitors?" I asked myself. I saw the evil in men, the horror of war, and human beings' defiance of righteousness. I was thirteen years old.

A Life after Liberation

My grandfather and father provided livelihoods to generations of families in Haeryong and the small farming towns that surrounded it.

Everyone was grateful to the Bai family. They looked upon Grandfather as their guardian, provider, and civic leader, which might explain why they protected our family from the guerrillas.

Soon after the liberation from Japan, our lives began to return to normal. But Father knew it would not last very long.

Ham Kyung Book-Do province, with three million people, held a student music competition in its capital of Chongjin. Haeryong participated, and my school selected me as its vocal contestant.

Our school's music director, Yoon Sung-Gyu, who had studied at the Leningrad Tchaikovsky Conservatory, taught me two songs—the aria "La Donna e Mobile" from Verdi's *Rigoletto*, with lyrics translated into Korean, and a Korean song he composed, "My Country, My Home."

After weeks of practice, my teacher and I left for Chongjin the day before the contest. Director Yoon kept the train cabin window closed and covered my face with a soft cloth every time the train passed through the many smoke-filled tunnels on the way. He was concerned I might catch a cold and lose my voice.

The contest took place in a large civic auditorium filled with a thousand people from many provincial cities and towns. My teacher and I waited backstage with eleven other contestants. Suddenly, Director Yoon broke open a raw egg and forced me to swallow it. He later told me that the egg helped clear my throat and helped me to sing vibrantly.

Then he slapped me on my back and turned me to the stage. "It's your turn," he said. I stood in front of a microphone, adjusted to my height, but I could not see the audience because of the single stage light pointed at my face.

I sang "La Donna e Mobile" first, and when I finished, I heard loud applause.

During my second song, "My Country, My Home," I forgot one line in the lyrics. I froze momentarily but recovered to finish the piece. I felt terrible for disappointing my teacher, family, school, and the people of my hometown. I wanted to cry, but for some reason, I did not.

When the selection committee announced the first-place winner, the entire audience groaned its disapproval. They awarded me second place. On the train ride back, Director Yoon comforted me. "You did wonderfully. I was pleased by how well you sang 'La Donna e Mobile'," he said.

When I returned to school the following day, I was overwhelmed to find the principal, teachers, and student body lined up waiting to hear me sing. The principal said the entire school was proud of my performance at the contest, then asked me to sing "La Donna e Mobile."

When I finished both songs, the entire audience of students and teachers burst into loud applause. I felt like a first-prize winner.

Later that evening, I sang "La Donna e Mobile" for my family, the workers on our estate, and a few neighbors. I saw my father was pleased. Even today, whenever I sing "La Donna e Mobile," I feel free.

The English translation of the Italian lyrics start:

A woman is a fickle
Like a feather in the wind
She changes her voice—and her mind
Always sweet, Pretty face
In tears or laughter—she is always lying

My music director Yoon translated it into Korean:

She is like a butterfly in the spring breeze
Butterfly, where are you going?
I wish to fly with you, my love, to eternity
never come back, just two of us

✍

Sensing the young communist revolutionaries would come someday to execute him, my father in 1947 decided to move the family to Wonsan, a port city of about 175,000 on the Sea of Japan, known to Koreans as the East Sea, just over two hundred miles south of Haeryong, where he had a large apple farm.

Wonsan spread along a beautiful, white sandy beach and was known for its warm ocean climate, delicious apples, and flavorful flounders caught off the coast. Its water along the shoreline was so clear that I could see shining pebbles and colorful little fish below on the sandy bottom. After school, I would walk the beach and swim all afternoon in summer.

My father's factory packed apples in wooden crates and exported them to Russia. To earn spending money, I worked with factory workers to make crates using pre-cut pieces of pine under the scorching sun at the packing yard until I could no longer hold a hammer because of blisters on my fingers.

I hid my entire summer's pay under a roof tile, but I made a mistake by telling my best friend where I hid it. He stole my money.

He was a year older and much bigger than I was. He thought he could get away with it. I chased him with my brother Ben's baseball bat and got him to apologize. I took back the stolen money, less a small amount he had already spent. I forgave him.

၅

Our dog at our apple farm, a big black German shepherd we called Gomi, was the size of a donkey and a faithful friend. We used a leash tied to a long chain tethered to a wire that allowed him to run along the length of our yard unencumbered. Gomi barked and tried to bite anyone who approached him except me. Gomi hugged me and licked my face until I begged him to stop.

၅

After two years in Wonsan, my father moved 130 miles west to Pyongyang, the capital city of North Korea, to manage his expanding business and stay farther away from young communist revolutionaries in Haeryong. He left the rest of the family behind in Wonsan.

Three years after the Japanese surrender, in 1948, the Korean peninsula was divided along the 38th parallel, creating the US-controlled Republic of Korea in the South and the new regime of the Democratic People's Republic of Korea in the North.

In 1948, my mother sent me to live with my father in Pyongyang. I stayed with him for one year, but we rarely spent time together because he was occupied all day at the office and then entertained government officials in the evening.

In the winter, I spent my time skating on the Dai Dong River that runs through Pyongyang, eating Naem Myung (cold noodles) at a neighborhood restaurant, and enjoying roasted chestnuts from outdoor street vendors.

When the boys in my new school saw me wearing a cashmere coat, they ridiculed me, calling me "bourgeois," and one day threw snowballs at me, some with stones inside. So, I went to school without that coat the next day, although I felt cold all day.

⁊

The day before Independence Day, August 15, our teacher gathered all the boys in his classroom and inducted us into the Communist Party. My teacher placed a red scarf around my neck and shook my hand. I became a communist at twelve and a half.

The next day I joined hundreds of thousands of students, all wearing red scarves, preparing to parade through Kim Il Sung Square. As the sun rose, we were standing ready, lining up at our designated spot on the hot concrete, waiting hours for the march to begin.

As the parade passed the reviewing stand, I saw the Great Leader Kim Il Sung for the first time in the far distance. The sun was setting when the parade ended, and we were all tired, thirsty, and hungry. As I walked the long way home alone, I began to understand what it was like to be a communist.

⁊

I was happy when my mother and the rest of the family joined us in Pyongyang. My brother Ben begged to stay in Wonsan. Mother knew nothing could take Ben away from his baseball team. Carl was in Seoul, attending high school, unable to come home because of the 38th parallel dividing North from South Korea. For two years, we had peaceful lives in Pyongyang.

But another war was about to begin.

CHAPTER FOUR

A New War Dawns

As dawn broke on a rainy Sunday morning, June 25, 1950, the army of the Democratic People's Republic of Korea opened fire on South Korean forces stationed along the 38th parallel. It was the start of an invasion of the South.

The next day, I heard the blaring announcements from a propaganda van moving slowly through the streets of Pyongyang, that seventy-five thousand of their brave soldiers crossed the 38th parallel to chase the US imperialists out of the country and to liberate the South.

That evening, my father gathered us and told us about what the United States and its allies had done after the Second World War, the significance of the day's announcement, and what it meant to Korea and our family.

After the war, the departure of the defeated Japanese removed their suffocating presence from Korea. However, it also created a power vacuum, an uneasy peace, and an ominous struggle to control the entire Korean peninsula. Korea would become the world's next stage for the battle between West and East, democracy and communism.

Soviet soldiers came only to the northeastern-most area of Korea, Ham Kyung Book-Do province, where we lived, without firing a shot. They left quickly and had no influence in North Korea when the country was created. When the Korean War began, there was no Russian or Chinese presence in North Korea.

According to many reports, North Korean independence fighters alone created the Democratic People's Republic of Korea. There are no Chinese or Russian soldiers in North Korea, then and today.

Rather than shooting, the Russian instead instilled its communist ideology on the newly created North Korean regime while the Americans fought in the Pacific leaving three hundred thousand of its young men and women killed or wounded.

The Soviet Union did play a significant, covert role in the conflict. It provided materials, medical services, and its efficient and deadly jet fighter, the MIG-15, to aid North Korean and Chinese forces against the United Nations, primarily Americans. Each would claim to be the legitimate government of all of Korea.

My father explained that during World War II, Kim Il Sung, the man I had seen on the Independence Day reviewing stand the summer before, had been a young revolutionary fighter, a hero of the anti-Japanese resistance. Kim Il Sung, my father continued, joined the anti-Japanese resistance at age fourteen in 1926 and for twenty years fought to liberate Korea, inspired by his hatred of the Japanese.

He would become the leader of the newly created Democratic People's Republic of Korea and install as a guiding principle, Juche, an ideal calling for self-reliance and autonomy. At the same time, the victorious Allied powers, including the United States under General Douglas MacArthur, established the South Korean government and named Lee Sung Man as its president.

The elements of a great conflict were in place.

The North Korean army took one week to take control of Seoul and one month to reach the Nak Dong River in the southeast corner of the peninsula. Soon after, the United States joined the war, followed by twenty-one countries of the United Nations. The non-US forces eventually contributed 10 percent of the total allied military forces.

On September 15, 1950, after two months of fierce fighting between the North and US-South Korean forces, the US Eighth

Army, led by General MacArthur, successfully landed at Inchon harbor, seventeen miles west of Seoul and halfway up the peninsula. It was a major allied military victory, second in scope only to the Normandy landing, cutting off the North Korean forces' supply lines.

The war would soon find its way to our backyard.

My father predicted the US-South Korean armies would take Pyongyang and continue to drive north and push the North Korean army off the land. Expecting a heavy air attack from the United States, my father directed his workers to build a giant wooden pyramid from massive rough-hewn logs in our yard. Then the workers dug out the ground beneath the pyramid and reinforced it with more timbers, creating a bomb shelter.

The night after they finished their work, a massive air raid sent my family scrambling down to the shelter. The ground under the pyramid shook violently with each explosion, which sent large shards of wood raining down on our heads and shoulders like subterranean missiles.

The pounding filled the air in the darkened shelter with dust, forcing us to cover our mouths with clothing to keep us from gagging and coughing. Over the intensified sound of the bombing, I could see the specks of dust falling on my mother's bowed head. The loud sound of bomb explosions made it so we could barely hear Mother's prayer to God in the dark.

She embraced the three of us, trying to deflect the pieces of timber that continued to drop on our heads as the bombs pounded the city with no sign of stopping. After the relentless and massive night-long bombing, our entire neighborhood suddenly became deadly silent.

The cries of women piercing the quiet night air in the distance soon broke the silence. It was apparent that South Korean soldiers were raping them.

At sunrise, I went out to the backyard and saw an enormous bomb crater just a few yards from the wooden pyramid where we had spent the horrible night. God had answered my mother's prayers and saved us.

Suddenly, I heard an earth-shaking roar coming from the nearby main street. I ran out to join other kids to watch US military tanks rolling down the streets. It was my first sight of American soldiers.

Several soldiers were sitting atop the tanks with bandoliers packed with ammunition across their hairy chests. Some were dark colored, another first for me. All were smoking cigars as they tossed chocolates and packs of chewing gum at us. It was my first experience with chewing gum. I swallowed it, thinking it was candy.

I thought of the crude, ill-behaved, savage Russian soldiers, the "Russkies" who had raped our maid. These soldiers looked different, taller and bigger, with different skin tones and hairstyles. They were nonchalant, but they all smiled at us, a stark contrast to the grim and unsmiling Russians I had seen earlier.

I saw white and black soldiers together, like good friends, flashing the same happy smiles. I wondered what kinds of people Americans were. "These men must have families," I thought. "They came from far away from their home to fight the battle, risking their lives, killing, and being killed in a strange country."

In contrast to what I had been taught, I did not see American soldiers as ruthless killers. Instead, they seemed friendly, and I was not frightened by them.

It was September 1950, and I had just turned thirteen years old.

CHAPTER FIVE

A Daunting Mission

With the American bombing campaign escalating, our family moved to Go-Chon, a small town of fewer than fifty people living in a cluster of some several houses with straw roofs, about thirty miles south of Pyongyang.

As soon as we settled in Go-Chon, my two-year-old sister Jung Ok, pretty and always joyful, became seriously ill. She grew thin and gaunt, and her pale skin became sunken on her face to the extent that I could see her bones protruding. She was so weak that she could not even cry; she just looked at me with big, open eyes and with no expression.

In such a remote area, there were no medical clinics or doctors. My father was helpless and would pierce Jung Ok's forehead with a large needle, trying to drain blood, hoping to revive her. It was difficult for me to see my baby sister having to endure such unbearable pain. I wished that she did not have any sensations left in her body to feel the pain.

My father had heard that a miracle drug, called penicillin, would save Jung Ok. He told me to go to his office in west Pyongyang and ask his plant manager, Mr. Kim, to get that penicillin. Since my two older brothers were hundreds of miles away, the responsibility fell on me.

My mother covered me with a blanket the night before I left the house and said, "Joon, sleep well. You will have a long journey to the city tomorrow." I left the house at sunrise with a jug of water and two rice balls wrapped in dry seaweed.

To reach the city early, I chose to walk through heavily wooded mountains, the shorter, most direct route. With no trails or signs, I followed the sun. I wanted to make sure I could return along the same path, so I blazed a trail by carving a two-inch X on the trunks of several tall trees to follow on the way back home.

As I entered Pyongyang in the late afternoon, sirens suddenly blared, and I saw hundreds of people scattering and running to designated underground bomb shelters, far below where I was standing.

When I heard an overhead roar, I looked up and saw thousands of tiny black objects like poppy seeds dropping from large planes that were falling toward me out of the blue sky. I quickly realized that those poppy seeds were bombs that appeared to be aimed directly at me.

It seemed impossible, but I did not have time to think about it. Nonetheless, I rushed to a large house nearby. Its gate was locked with sets of large, black metal rings. I leaned against the corner of a wooden fence post and the gate, crouched, shut my eyes, and covered my head with my hands.

The whistling of the falling bombs was followed immediately by the sonic impact of the explosions once they hit the ground. I shuddered and became numb with the concussive force of the pounding. The gate trembled with each blast, so I leaned onto the wooden post to keep from falling.

I do not remember how long the raid lasted, but when it stopped, I felt the heat and smelled burning wood. I opened my eyes and saw dozens of bomb fragments, black pieces bigger than my palm, still hot, had pierced the wooden gate, forming a silhouette of my crouching shape. It was as if a circus knife-thrower had hurled his wares directly at me. I could not believe how many bomb fragments, still smoking and burning, had missed me by inches.

At a second siren, I saw citizens emerging from the shelters and begin to clean the debris from the streets. First, they swept broken concrete and shattered wood into two-wheel trolleys using their hands and straw brooms, then carried the debris away.

I noticed they recovered from the bombing quickly and returned to their everyday lives. The lesson I learned from the citizens of Pyongyang that afternoon was that the Juche ideology informed the steely resolve of North Koreans.

I saw in that Juche spirit that they would never be defeated. "We can win over imperial aggressors," groups chanted as they marched through the streets.

At last, I arrived at my father's factory. A few workers greeted me warmly and told me that they saw more than one hundred B-52s had dropped thousands of bombs on the west side of Pyongyang, where I was. When I found Mr. Kim, the factory manager, and asked him about penicillin, he said he had not heard of it. I was dumbstruck, frozen by his remark, and could not accept his words.

They gave me a bowl of rice and bean straw soup, and I went into a room next to the office to sleep on the warm floor with a wooden pillow and a small blanket. I lay awake, staring at the bright moon through a small window, thinking about Jung Ok.

I returned to Go-Chon empty-handed, reversing my route of the preceding day. The way back seemed far more exhausting.

Two days later, Jung Ok died.

I made a coffin with wood I had found in our next-door neighbor's barn. My mother and I wrapped my sister in a white bedsheet. I told my heartbroken father to stay home and comfort my mother.

An old farmer next door and I carried the coffin to a nearby hill in the cold morning air and buried Jung Ok. As we spread the last bit of soil on the grave, the sun rose to lift the morning fog. The farmer left, but I sat by her grave all day, not believing Jung Ok was dead.

When the sun set on the hill, my mother came and said, "Let us go home. Jung Ok is resting in peace." We sat and cried until it became dark.

I could not sleep that night, worrying Jung Ok would be cold in the morning. I went by her grave every day until our family left Go-Chon. I would sit there all day believing she would appear again with her pretty, smiling face.

For the first time, I felt the deep sorrow of losing a loved one.

CHAPTER SIX

Escape

Daily life quieted as Allied forces took control of Pyongyang and pushed the North Korean army farther to the north, allowing us to move back to our house. As we rode an ox-driven carriage back to Pyongyang, I kept looking back toward Jung Ok's gravesite.

"Jung Ok, I will be back," I told her.

∽

When he was thirteen years old, my brother Carl had left the family to attend high school in Seoul, staying with our grandfather. The division of Korea along the 38th parallel marooned him there, unable to return home.

As an eighteen-year-old high school senior in Seoul, he was conscripted into the South Korean Army, which desperately needed soldiers. Young men would be lured to theaters by the promise of free movies, forcibly abducted, brought to a training camp, and assigned to a student regiment.

An odd bit of luck would bring Carl to Pyongyang. He learned that our niece, Soo Ok, was dating a South Korean Special Forces colonel, Choi Moo Ryong, whose battalion was getting ready to head north. He planned to take Soo Ok with him, so Carl asked to join them.

My mother and Carl had a tearful and joyous reunion. After a two-day stay with our family, Carl had to leave Pyongyang with the colonel.

∽

On October 25, 1950, the war escalated.

Allied troops, predominantly US Army, reinforcing the South Korean Army, approached the Sino-North Korean border and met with a massive Chinese Army force, which had launched a major surprise offense.

By mid-November, the advancing Chinese Army, numbered close to a million troops, forced the US Eighth Army to retreat as they closed in on Pyongyang. Once again, we heard explosions. This time, we saw and heard hundreds of frequent staccato bursts of explosions accompanied by hundreds of fireballs lighting up the Pyongyang sky with earth-shaking sounds, like the finale of Tchaikovsky's "1812 Overture."

The US Army, as they were retreating from Pyongyang, set fire to hundreds of fifty-five-gallon steel fuel drums at an ammunition depot. The drums shot into the dark sky and exploded in a fearsome display. The sky was painted blood-red, dripping in a menacing display of fire and brimstone in a wild specter, unlike any fireworks I could have imagined.

Once again, we were caught in what looked and sounded like a cataclysmic event. Talk in the neighborhood spread that the United States would drop an atomic bomb on Pyongyang as it did on the Japanese cities of Hiroshima and Nagasaki.

Father told us we had to leave Pyongyang for a few days to escape the atomic bomb. We packed blankets and enough food for one week and headed to the south.

With my eight-year-old sister, Chung Sook, holding my mother's hand and my six-year-old brother, Ken, clutching my father's hand, we began to walk. It was late November 1950.

I carried blankets, two cooking pans dangling from my backpack, and a box of corn flakes left behind by American soldiers. My father grabbed bags of rice, some dried foods, and a jug of water. We did not know we were embarking on a six-week journey.

We joined a short line of refugees walking in the falling snow on a narrow country road. As more snow fell, the line grew longer by the hour. The women bore large bundles of provisions balanced on their heads, and some men and women pushed two-wheel trolleys.

After a few days of endless walking, our shoes split, and our socks tore. I remember looking down and seeing my toes protruding from my shoes. I covered my freezing feet with rags to prevent frostbite. We constantly moved to stay warm.

Some farmhouses along the route were heavily locked to keep refugees from entering. Others displayed pine-tree wreaths, indicating a newborn child within. An old Korean tradition prohibits anyone from visiting a house with a newborn baby.

Often, we would find an open gate on farmhouses only to discover refugees already occupied it. We would have to sleep in the barn. On several occasions, we found shelter in barren hillside caves to prevent us from freezing.

My sister and brother and I cradled against each other for warmth, but the piercing wind would rob us of whatever body heat we could generate. The moonlight would occasionally break through the dark clouds, a sign it would turn to snow, our constant worry.

One day, we spotted a well. We were about to lower the bucket when we saw the bloated body of a dead South Korean soldier floating.

On another occasion, walking ahead of my family, I picked up a can of corn beef hash that the retreating Americans had discarded. I was about to put my finger in to scoop out the contents when I saw it was full of white maggots. I could not eat it though I was starving.

The trek seemed unrelenting.

We watched refugees bury their babies who had died from cold and hunger. Parents buried dead children quickly and returned to marching forward, taking little time to grieve because North Korean armies were approaching us from behind.

It all happened within short time. I saw the mother of a baby move her feet forward as if she was carrying a ton of earth. I thought it was so devastating and painful; she did not even cry, just looked down and plodded ahead carrying her shattered heart.

The Eighth Army continued to bomb the roads and bridges as they passed to slow down the advancing North Korean soldiers.

Once, we came to a frozen river to find the ice was not quite thick enough to cross on foot. We had to wait for hours in a long line for a few tiny rowboats to take us across. Finally, watching people on a rail bridge that had been heavily damaged by bombs, I thought I could join them and cross the river.

Mother kept asking me not to, but I convinced her I would be fine. I went to the bridge and joined with hundreds of men who were climbing precariously over the long span. I stepped on the bent rails and broken wooden trestles, hanging on to heavy, thick ropes others had left earlier. A few men slipped and fell off the bridge, crashing into the river. I made it to the other side and waited for my family to arrive.

Exhausted from the journey, which covered nearly 240 frozen miles, crossing a temporary bridge over the Han River, at last, we arrived in Seoul.

CHAPTER SEVEN

Busan

We were too exhausted to feel even the slightest wave of elation from having survived our ordeal, and arrived in Seoul believing our strenuous trek had ended.

We headed to our grandfather's house, anticipating a tearful reunion and an opportunity, finally, to have warm food and a chance to sleep comfortably indoors.

Instead, when we arrived, we found the house was locked. Our distant relative Kum Soon, who lived next door, opened the door for us and told us that Grandfather had simply disappeared one night, and that, soon after, the rest of the family had left. We were confronted with a mystery that remains unsolved even today, more than seventy years later; our beloved grandfather had vanished.

Dead tired, we quickly fell asleep, snoring but not knowing our arduous journey would continue. As I was falling asleep, I saw Mother, tired and struggling to remain sitting up, staying awake to thread a needle to mend our socks.

The next day, we learned from other neighbors that hundreds of notable scientists, prosperous people in business, and community leaders were all kidnapped to Pyongyang by North Korean intelligence agents. We sat together and prayed for our grandfather to return home safely and soon.

To our shocking disappointment, we quickly discovered that many people in Seoul had fled farther southeast to the port city of Busan, Korea's second-largest city after Seoul, two hundred miles away on the East Sea.

The next day, Father told us that we must continue to escape to Busan. The city had become a beacon for refugees fleeing the bombings and death and daily combat that had disrupted their once peaceful and prosperous lives.

We quickly packed food, changed into clean clothes, and headed to the Seoul railroad station, where we climbed aboard an open cargo train, joining hundreds of other refugees. The train was pulled by a coal-fired locomotive, and our car was powdered with coal dust and packed with refugees, leaving us little room to stand or sit.

The train stopped periodically under the water tanks for the refilling necessary to produce the steam needed to power the locomotive. At each stop, refugees jumped from the train, collected small tree branches and sticks near the track, then lit cooking fires for what little food they had brought along. They would eat quickly as the train replenished its water and got ready to move again.

At one stop, two US military policemen burst from the train's passenger compartment, rushed to the newly lit fires, and kicked over the pots and pans, knocking the food to the ground. I was shocked by what appeared to be a heartless act.

Later I realized the MPs were afraid sparks from the fires could ignite the fuel and ammunition in the train's military cargo. Still, I questioned why. Why couldn't they see we were starving and traveling on empty stomachs?

I felt sad and helpless to see my sister Chung Sook and brother Ken stoically enduring terrible hunger during our train ride. Yet, they displayed remarkable courage, never complained, cried, or asked for things we did not have. I was immensely proud of them. Those two siblings, so young, gave me the courage to act as big brother.

Unexpectedly, the train stopped in the middle of a long tunnel, trapping us with fumes, which quickly became overwhelming. We had to cover our faces with handkerchiefs, towels, or any cloth we could find to keep the smoke from filling our lungs. When the train emerged from the tunnel after about an hour, our faces were blackened by soot, our eyes and teeth white in sharp contrast.

Over the sound of the locomotive's whistle, we heard the heart-breaking cry of a mother holding her dead baby, and saw tears dropping down her soot-caked face like black ink. Many of us prayed for the baby and the mother; some wept.

A few men jumped from the train at the next train stop. Using metal pans and their bare hands, they dug out enough dirt for a make-shift grave. Then they gently laid the baby into it and covered its tiny body with rocks and gravel.

The train began to move again, carrying with it the mournful sound of the mother's weeping and the clack of metal wheels against the rail, and sped to Busan.

After three days of many long stops, we finally pulled into Busan station, a big, red brick building with a pointed clock tower. We stepped gingerly from the train and tried to enter the station. We quickly found out that the place was so packed with refugees that we could not put one foot inside.

We had to stay outdoors, in the yard behind the station building, in the bitter cold. As the evening approached, I noticed large cardboard packing boxes, Gaylord boxes, scattered around the station yard. I collected a couple of them and rigged up a temporary shelter to protect us from the bone-chilling wind. My father told me I was ingenious.

The first night, the sky was full of stars with a bright moon. It was unbearably cold, and I could not sleep. I wandered away from the station and came upon a shabby kitchen in a narrow backstreet, filled with steam from a large boiling pot.

I could barely make out a woman inside using a cleaver to cut an octopus on a wooden chopping block. She served a plate full of octopus to two dirty and disheveled young men sitting at the table drinking soju, a robust Korean liquor.

They blew on the hot octopus and chewed it as if they had not eaten for days. I thought about storming inside and stealing a bite.

It was January 1, 1951, New Year's Day. I was thirteen years and four months old.

CHAPTER EIGHT

Surviving in Busan

There were signs that Busan would be less chaotic and, perhaps, safer, though the war continued around us.

I spotted a large white ship emblazoned with a large red cross in Busan harbor. It was part of the Swedish Red Cross Field Hospital in Busan, the first medical unit of the war.

Sweden had dispatched medical units and operated the hospital. Norway set up its Mobile Army Surgical Hospital, and Denmark sent the *Jutlandia*, a hospital ship, to provide emergency surgery to thousands of war victims, civilians, and soldiers.

Like hundreds of thousands of war-torn families in the city, we began a needle-in-a-haystack search for Ben and Carl. We placed posters up and down many busy streets that read: "Looking for Bai Byung Sup and Bai Byung Jin."

Three days later, a miracle happened. My mother spotted Ben in the mingling crowd in front of the United States Information Service building. She gasped and rushed to a skinny boy with long, dirty hair, calling him, "Byung Jin, Byung Jin, my son." She then hugged the hardly recognizable boy, who stood shocked, staring at Mother. I watched the sadness and a deep yearning born of a long separation suddenly blossom with happiness in a joyous flash.

Ben told us he had left Wonsan, went to Hungnam port on an open truck with other refugees, and boarded the *Meredith Victory*, a US merchant marine freighter built to transport supplies and equipment during the Second World War.

Designed to carry a crew of fifty-nine, the *Meredith Victory*, under the command of Captain Leonard LaRue, would perform what has been called the most significant humanitarian rescue operation in history in December 1950. Later dubbed the "Ship of Miracles," its crew evacuated fourteen thousand refugees fleeing from the advancing massive Chinese Army from upper North Korea to Geoje Island near Busan.

Ben, fifteen years old, was among the passengers cramped on the open deck, packed like sardines, with barely enough room to move as they sat shoulder-to-shoulder in freezing sea air during the three-day voyage.

Captain LaRue later said, "There's no explanation for why refugees, as stoic as they are, were able to stand virtually motionless and in silence. We were impressed by the conduct of the refugees, despite their desperate plight. We were touched by it."

Ben told us that he and other refugees were so hungry they pushed each other away to dip their hands in boiling water to take a handful of Su-Je-Bi in searing pain.

Su-Je-Bi is wheat flour made into dough, pulled in thumb size, and boiled in salted water. Later called "refugee's food," it is like a Chinese dumpling, without fillings. It is usually cooked in meat and fish broth, but the ship did not carry enough food to feed fourteen thousand unexpected passengers and refugees. Ben told us that no one died, but five babies were born on the main deck during a three-days voyage.

Father had hidden a chest full of diamonds, which he had received from Russians in exchange for apples exported from his farm, in the basement of our house in Wonsan. There was no currency exchange during the war. The only acceptable payment for the goods received were luxurious commodities like diamonds.

My parents were surprised to see Ben had brought with him only two large diamonds and his prize possession, a baseball glove. Father was disappointed Ben did not bring more, but he understood Ben would have suffered if other refugees learned he was carrying diamonds.

The miracles would continue.

Days after our reunion with Ben, Carl found us through relatives, my mother's two sisters, who lived in a harbor city, Jin Hae, home of the Korean Naval Academy. My mother was overjoyed to see her oldest son again.

A year later, Carl volunteered to enter Korean Naval Academy, where he graduated and became a naval officer. He served as the captain of a Korean Navy anti-submarine chaser, PC-461, for seven years before he retired. Carl told us that before he left Pyongyang, Colonel Choi, the man our cousin was dating, helped him join the South Korean special forces battalion he commanded as it was moving north.

Soon after, Carl became sick, and his platoon left him behind in Dae-Jung City. He changed into civilian clothes, then drifted through the countryside, begging for food, staying at different houses night after night. He finally arrived in Jin Hae, still sick, and found our two aunts on Mother's side.

With one diamond, father purchased a small weather-worn house at the base of Mount Yu Dock in northwestern Busan near the US Army camp. The second diamond brought us enough money to sustain ourselves for a short time.

I knew I had to do something to help my family.

At first, I thought about shining shoes for the US soldiers at the nearby camp. Then, I learned that the base post exchange (PX) sold cigarettes by the carton. Many soldiers who were frequently shipped out for day duty or to the city for enjoyment did not want to carry an entire carton; they wanted only a single pack. I thought that I could start a small enterprise, and I set up a shop.

First, I made a wooden tray and legs from discarded crates to display the goods, and found another crate to sit on at the corner of a crossroad, where I found the heaviest traffic. Then I bought cartons of Lucky Strikes, Camels, and Chesterfields from the soldiers, and candy like SweeTarts and Life Savers, chocolates like Milkas and Hershey bars, and Wrigley's chewing gum. I sold the cigarettes by the pack and made a 10 percent profit.

I never felt shame for being a cigarette boy on the street nor questioned why my elder brothers did not give me any relief. Because there was no school while the country was in the refugee state, I ran this business for an entire year, from early in the morning until late afternoon in the rain and snow.

My mother always brought an umbrella at the first sign of inclement weather. At times I would wait hours to sell anything, but I restrained myself from the temptation of eating even one piece of candy. Instead, I gave all my earnings to my mother to help buy food.

Every day she helped me take the stand back home. As we trudged home, she rarely spoke, but I knew how proud she was of me and how painful it was for her to see me sitting all day under the sun by the road. I felt heartwarming love from my mother every time we walked home together.

Later, at our family reunions, Carl often said to the family, "When I saw Joon standing on the street selling cigarettes, I noticed his enduring character. I knew then that Joon someday would become a successful businessman like our grandfather."

The seesawing battles between North Korea-Chinese forces and South Korea-UN allies continued until 1953. Finally, after so much fighting and disruption and death, the situation ended as it began three years earlier. An armistice agreement was signed on July 27, 1953, dividing Korea into two again.

Today, in 2021, it is unbelievable that neither side has signed a peace treaty.

CHAPTER NINE

Off to America

My mother dedicated herself to provide to Ben and me the best education possible.

My grandfather had been president of the parent association at the prestigious Kyung-Gi High School in Seoul before the war and had funded a new school auditorium. Thanks to our grandfather's contribution, Ben and I were admitted into the Busan branch campus. The Busan campus was comprised of army tents, under which the students sat on flat boulders, rain or snow. But décor aside, the education offered by dedicated teachers was superb.

After the armistice was declared, the Busan campus closed and moved to Seoul. At the same time, my father's trading business improved, which allowed our family to move to an old house near the capitol building in Seoul. Ben and I continued our schooling and eventually graduated from Kyung-Gi High School.

∽

Our stay in Busan ignited for me a lifelong love of movies. I would regularly go to a film's first screening on its opening day, where I'd excitedly stare at the giant promotional posters for the day's movie. I'd go early to watch previews of the US Army news, Fox Movie-Tone, and Warner Brothers cartoons featuring the Road Runner and Bugs Bunny before the main feature film started.

I memorized the tunes and lyrics of each film's title song: Gene Kelly and "Singing in the Rain," Doris Day and "Que Sera, Sera," the Four Aces and "Three Coins in the Fountain."

I loved post-Second World War films directed by great filmmakers like Vittorio De Sica, Billy Wilder, Orson Welles, William Wyler, David Lean, and others.

Not content to simply watch the movies, I would also devour and memorize the short biographies of the leading actors and production crew members in the promotional fliers the theater handed out.

Afterward, I would entertain my friends by telling them the movie's plot and singing the title song. They enjoyed hearing about the new film and would learn to sing theme songs from me. Those movies brought real-life questions and inspiration to me as a teenage boy in Korea, and they would continue to do so even as I grew older.

I was touched by the character of Robert Jordan, played by Gary Cooper, in *For Whom the Bell Tolls*. Jordan, an idealistic young American fighting in the Spanish Civil War, gave up his life to protect the freedom of the people of Spain and to save Spanish guerrilla Maria, his love. I was impressed with the message that ideals and love are worthy of a man's life.

I questioned what David Lean was attempting to convey to viewers in *The Bridge on the River Kwai*. Was it about the folly of pride? Was it a battle between two stubborn men, the British Colonel Nicholson and the Japanese Colonel Saito? Was it the effect of brainwashing? Or the folly of Nicholson's obsession with building a bridge and not realizing the overriding goal was winning the war?

Nicholson realizes his mistake too late and asks, at the film's conclusion, "What have I done?" I wondered how many evil leaders of humankind would say that.

Much later, I would learn in the film *Papillion* that a man's will would win over the power of oppression. And I would also later see the magnificent power of love in *Dr. Zhivago* and *Wuthering Heights*. These wonderful films would prompt me to ask myself deeper questions.

What is the nature of love?

To what extent can a person love another?

What is the ultimate power of love?

These films affected me deeply, and they still do. It is a beautiful statement on the power of movies to motivate, inspire, and educate while offering wonderful entertainment. Movies introduced me to American culture, its ideals and philosophies, etiquettes, and the meaning of human rights. I began to dream about going to America to experience what I saw in films and pursue a college education.

ᔕ

Ben had become a star baseball player as a pitcher and clean-up hitter when he was just a sophomore in high school. He took his team to the Korean National High School Baseball Tournament's final.

He went to the United States as an exchange student in 1957, enrolling at Northwest Missouri State College, the same college I would attend when I came to America. Ben later transferred to North Park College in Chicago, and in his junior year, he married a Korean student, Charlene Jang. They graduated and settled in Chicago and had a daughter, Susan, in 1959.

That same year, Charlene, while attending Mary Hardin Baylor College in Belton, Texas, asked Pastor M.E. McGlamery of Hampton Place Baptist Church, with a congregation of two thousand members, in Dallas, to sponsor me.

The sponsorship called for the church to be responsible for me while I was a student in the States, though it did not pay for my tuition or living expenses. The church sponsored my application to come to the United States as an exchange student under the Fulbright Foreign Student Exchange Program.

In 1946, Senator William Fulbright of Arkansas wrote the bill passed by Congress that would result in what became known as the Fulbright Scholarships, one of the most widely recognized and prestigious scholarships globally. It opened the door for young people to share ideas, knowledge, and culture worldwide.

I was one of the beneficiaries.

To meet the mandatory requirement for students leaving Korea to study abroad, I had to pass a nationwide examination and serve eighteen months of South Korean military duty.

As part of my military service, I had to complete a grueling three months of vigorous training at a camp, Yong San, a hundred miles south of Seoul in the harshness of winter, from November through January.

Our main diet consisted of brown rice with a small bowl of soup with a few strings of bean sprouts floating in warm salted water. We had less than one minute to finish meals, just long enough for our sergeant to make one complete turn as he stood and stared at us eating. We would take cold showers outside in freezing temperatures.

After completing training, I was assigned to the transportation division of the Seventh Army near the Demilitarized Zone (DMZ), the infamous no-man's land established after the armistice that would become the scene of continued tensions over the years between North and South.

The morning after we arrived at the camp, someone stole truck tires from the storage facility. Our sergeant took four of us, all newly arrived privates, outside and ordered us to strip off our clothes except for our briefs. Then he had us stand barefoot in the gelid air, below freezing temperature, after which he forced us to stay in the push-up position for over thirty minutes.

While I was in the position, straining from the effort, I saw hundreds of black lice jumping up and down on my white undershirt, which I had placed on the ground in front of me. The lice were freezing to death.

Most days, we cleaned our rifles and went up the mountain nearby to bring back broken tree branches to heat the camp tents in those freezing winter days.

I completed my eighteen months of service uneventfully and was looking forward to seeing America.

When I returned home from the service, I found my family had moved to a small apartment. With his business beginning to fail, my father had sold our house. The first thing I wanted to do was go to the public bathhouse. There, I sat in a large pool of hot water for few minutes and found out, surprisingly, there was nothing to clean on my body. In the winter cold, my skin, which I had so rigorously rubbed with a cloth to rid myself of lice, was immaculate.

We did not have money for my airfare and travel expenses to America, so my mother went to relatives to borrow the money. I remember sitting in the living room corner of one of the relative's houses we visited, watching tears drop from my mother's eyes as she asked for help.

I agonized seeing how difficult it must have been for this proud woman. My mother compromised her pride and dignity for my future. My mother's love was embedded in my heart and has stayed with me always.

After a tearful farewell with my mother and my family, I left Seoul for America.

CHAPTER TEN

Coming to America

I will never forget September 13, 1959, the day I flew on an airplane for the first time and the day of my separation from my family, especially my beloved mother, who had sustained, supported, and loved me.

I slowly climbed the long flight of boarding stairs to the Korean Air Douglas DC-4 that would take me to America. I wanted to savor the experience, knowing it would be some time before I would see my family again.

As I reached the top of the boarding stairs, I stood for a second to look down on my family and my country. I had a lump in my throat, took a deep breath, and made my way to my window seat.

I looked at my family standing and waving near the departure gate to the side of the single runway in the dirt field of Seoul Yeouido International Airport. In the distance, I saw Mother was wiping tears with a white handkerchief.

I listened intently to the increasing pitch of the propellers on the four-engine plane as it taxied, accelerated, and lifted off, bound for Seattle and my new life. My mother disappeared in the distance.

Over the large, fluffy white clouds, I was washed with memories of our trying times, of growing up during the war, graduating high school, taking the scholarship examination, and serving in the military to arrive at this moment. I was carrying Mother's tearful face with me.

I hoped the dreams that had sprung from watching all the movies I loved so much would come true for me. Out the plane's window, I saw the wing cutting through thick white clouds in the blue sky. I closed my eyes and pinched my thigh, and told myself, "This is not a dream."

∽

Once the plane reached flying altitude and leveled off, I heard infants crying from behind the curtain that closed off the plane's rear section. Curious, I peeked and saw two dozen or so babies in wooden trays wrapped in soft cloths.

I opened the curtain and walked over to a man caring for the babies and introduced myself. The man had thick black eyebrows above a face dripping with sweat, a black mustache, and big eyes. Behind the man's face, I saw a warm heart.

The man told me he was Harry Holt from Oregon. With his wife, Bertha, and two nurses, he was bringing twenty Korean war orphans to America. Years later, I found out that Mr. Holt and his team became the pioneers of international adoptions.

I was tired and about to fall asleep, but the crying babies kept me awake, and I knew it would be a long flight. Again, I went to the back of the aircraft and noticed that the Holts and the nurses appeared exhausted, changing diapers, bottle-feeding the babies, holding them against their shoulders, and burping them. I asked Mr. Holt if I could assist in some way.

He thanked me and said I could change diapers for the babies. Then he showed me an easy way to do it, by lifting the baby's feet with my left hand, replacing the wet diaper with a dry one using my right, then wiping, powdering, and fastening the cloth with two large safety pins.

After changing two dozen diapers that night, I became an expert. Changing the diapers, I realized the babies, different colors, were flying above the vast Pacific Ocean, going to unknown places, and to mothers who they had not seen.

I thought this was another tragedy the war created. As I changed the diapers, I held each of baby's hands and prayed that they would find good lives and much happiness in the New World.

Then I returned to my seat, dead tired, and took the babies with me into my dreams. A voice on the speaker woke me up. The pilot announced that the flight we were on was Korean Air's inaugural Trans-Pacific flight and that we were flying over Alaska, which had recently become the forty-ninth state.

As the plane approached Alaska, the pilot announced that a mechanical problem called for an emergency landing at Shemya Air Force Base in the Aleutian Islands. Passengers enjoyed coffees and cookies in the lounges of an air force hangar. After a few hours, we took off again and landed in Seattle in the early morning of September 14, 1959.

I had a four-hour layover in Seattle before my Northwest Airlines flight to Chicago. Walking around the airport, I noticed a giant ad for Greyhound Bus posted on the window of a travel agency. I went into the office and exchanged my domestic flight tickets for a Greyhound bus ticket.

My desire to see America got my attention, perhaps, but the savings of forty-five dollars from exchanging airfare to bus tickets was too attractive not to take. I added my savings to the fifty dollars my mother put in my jacket when she hugged me at the airport. It was a considerable amount of money for me and made me feel secure.

The bus ride to Chicago would take two days. I ate four meals of large eighteen-cent pancakes, served around the clock at Greyhound depot restaurants. I did not know what to order on the menu, and I liked the pancakes.

About half a day into the ride, the bus stopped at Billings, Montana, and a gentle white-haired older lady got on board and sat next to me. She introduced herself as Mary Hayward and told me she was going to Minneapolis to attend her granddaughter's wedding.

Over a day-long bus ride, we talked endlessly about places in America, Korean culture, movies, our families, and what motivated me to come to America.

I was surprised to realize how well I spoke English. Many years of hard work studying English in high school was paying off.

When Mrs. Hayward boarded in Billings, she had gently placed a green hatbox in the open overhead storage rack above our seat. Whenever the bus hit a bump or made a sharp turn, she would stand up and check that the hatbox stayed in place. When the bus stopped in Minneapolis, I reached out and handed her the hatbox. She opened it and took out a beautiful green hat, matching the color of her eyes. She put on her hat and looked at her family waving at her through the window.

She turned and hugged me before joining them. "Good luck, Joon. You are an American now. Go make your dream a success," she told me. I watched from my bus seat as her granddaughter and the rest of her family embraced her, expressing their love for her and praising her beautiful hat. One more time, Mrs. Hayward looked back toward me and waved as she walked away from the bus to the family van.

We exchanged holiday cards until her family wrote to me that she had passed away during my junior year in college. I will never forget that bus ride across the Northwest with Mrs. Hayward. I did not tell her how beautiful she was when she departed the bus. I am sad today knowing that I would never be able to. I miss her sweet smile.

After over forty hours on the road, the bus finally arrived in Chicago at the Greyhound terminal at three o'clock in the morning. Ben and Charlene were there to greet me. I slept the entire first day at Ben's. The next day he took me to the discount shops on South Halsted Street in Chicago and bought me clothes I would need for school in the fall.

Ben and Charlene had a baby daughter, Susan. Ben worked at a bookstore on Chicago Avenue as a store manager and part-time as a night guard at a bank in South Side. Charlene was a dietician at the Wesley Memorial Hospital on Randolph Street. Like any other young married couple with a newborn baby, they worked hard to save for their future.

The next evening, I accompanied Ben to his bank job. He was wearing his security guard uniform, complete with a badge and pistol. We went out for snacks and found a group of Black men talking and laughing around a grill, cooking barbeque in front of a small grocery store at the corner of South Halsted and 106th Street. The mouthwatering aroma and flavorful smoke of baby back ribs filled the cool September air. A heavyset man, cooking the ribs and wearing a large apron, offered us a large chunk of ribs, and in return we bought a round of beer for everyone. The delicious ribs, cool beer, and the genial welcome by locals on that night remain a fond memory.

No one we met that night seemed to care if we were Asians, spoke with an accent, or what we were doing at that hour of the night in their neighborhood, which made me feel like I was one of them. Coming to America and being welcomed by people I had never met gave me a sense of peace. Two days later, it was time to go to school.

Ben and Charlene took me to the bus station to say farewell and wish me the best at school. Ben gave me fifty dollars from his savings. I bathed in my brother's love as I boarded the bus and waved goodbye to them.

The Continental Bus took me to Kansas City, where I transferred to another bus, and arrived in Maryville, Missouri, late in the night. Riding with a handful of passengers inside a dark bus, gazing out at the passing farmland, I prayed to God to grant me peace in a new school and new town and that hope lives within me still.

CHAPTER ELEVEN

Maryville

After a taxi dropped me on campus, I found my way to the large administration building, where Mr. Jones, the dean of students at Northwest Missouri State College, greeted me. His thick Southern accent was unlike any English I had heard, and I could not understand a word he was saying. I sat across from him at his desk and nodded, hoping to pick up some sort of clue as to what he was explaining.

Two days before classes began, the campus was empty except for a few basketball players practicing for a season-opening game. I met them in my dormitory hallway, towering around a soft-drink vending machine. I was amazed at their height as I stood next to them. One of them handed me a cold bottle of Coca-Cola, and I had my first taste of the quintessential American drink. I liked it. More so, I appreciated the tall basketball player's friendly gesture.

The next day, the foreign-student adviser showed me around campus and talked to me about courses I could take. I enrolled in a bachelor's degree program in liberal arts. I ate three meals each day for the first two days at the dormitory dining hall with just a few advanced students and the basketball players. Once the semester started, I joined a full dining room and watched in awe at boys consuming quarts of milk just for breakfast. The food, meals like thick pork with white beans, was not what I had grown up with. I realized why these farm boys were so big.

The first Homecoming was special. Candidates for the Homecoming Queen would greet me with, "Hi, there" as they passed by.

I thought they were saying, "Hi, dear."

The dining hall did not serve lunch or dinner on Sundays, but I learned that the First United Methodist Church in Maryville served free lunch to its congregation. I attended church there every Sunday, after which church folks invited me to their homes for dinner.

I had been introduced to Christianity through my mother's prayers, but I had not formally joined the faith. On November 15, 1959, I became a Christian after being baptized with a group of young men and women.

Conscious of expenses, I stayed at the dormitory for only one semester, then moved to a student apartment within walking distance of campus to save on living expenses. Ben continued to send twenty dollars every other week to support me.

I would shovel snow from the long and wide driveways of my elderly neighbors. They all paid me twenty-five cents for the work, but for some, I shoveled for free.

My freshman year at Northwest Missouri State College gave me the time to transition into my new and exciting life in America. It allowed me to get acquainted with the different culture and learn to prepare for my future.

During that first year, I was one of only a handful of Asians in Maryville. The townspeople—teachers, students, and school administrators—were all kind to me. I was especially grateful to the church and to the folks who fed me each Sunday, and to Mr. Gordon, the pharmacist and corner drugstore owner who gave me over-the-counter cold medications for free when I visited his store.

I would get up at five o'clock each morning to catch up on homework as I listened to country music from my bedside radio, music for the farmers heading to the fields.

My year in Maryville was an excellent experience, and an introduction to the sweet, calm, warm, friendly, caring, and peaceful rhythms of small-town America. I liked the music and the people I met in Missouri, the "Show Me State," with its Lake of the Ozarks, a giant reservoir in America's Heartland.

My student adviser had told me the United States was short of engineers and that I should consider engineering. By the end my freshman year, I switched majors and transferred to a highly competitive engineering college, Missouri School of Mines and Metallurgy, in Rolla.

CHAPTER TWELVE

The Pace Quickens

The academic program at Missouri School of Mines and Metallurgy was not designed for the weak at heart or for any student indifferent to studying.

In fact, the program was created to weed out those whose enthusiasm for rigorous academic work was less than total. There were about twelve co-eds in the entire student body of about two thousand, all cheerleaders. Regardless of how high they could jump, they cheered for a team that did not win a game that season.

It took five years for its students to graduate with 156 credit hours, compared to 125 hours for liberal art schools. Students, including me, did not have time for extra activities. When we were not in classrooms, we were at the mechanical engineering laboratories or applying civil engineering practices in the field.

My only relief from the relentless academic pace was trips to Chicago during Thanksgiving and Christmas breaks. There, I walked the length of Rush Street, a popular bar and restaurant row known for its vibrant nightlife, going door to door, from Chicago Avenue all the way to Pearson Street, looking for busboy or dishwasher jobs. I was always able to find work during the busy holiday season. Although I worked only a few days, I earned enough to pay for a month's groceries.

Every year, I would head to Chicago to work during summer vacation. One summer, I worked two jobs, assembling windows during the day at the Wind-Check company in suburban Addison and bussing tables in the evenings at the Pick Congress Hotel restaurant downtown on Michigan Avenue. I would get up at six o'clock and drive the twenty-plus miles out to the town of Addison, where I'd work until four. Then I'd drive back to the Congress. When the long day ended near midnight, I would go home and grab a short sleep before I'd do it all over again the next day.

When I arrived at the Congress, I would stop at a locker to quickly change into a white busboy uniform, head to the kitchen, and grab hot dinner rolls slathered with butter to bring up my energy.

The grand ballroom, located on the first floor, had a dance floor surrounded by dining tables. Bandleader Dick Sarlo played tenor saxophone and sang at the Congress for years, backed by his big band.

In the 1960s, he also led a band at the old Villa Venice in the Chicago suburb of Northbrook, and he opened shows for the famous Rat Pack, Dean Martin, Sammy Davis Jr., and Frank Sinatra.

Dick would come into the kitchen for a cup of coffee and a hot bun. He always tapped my shoulder. "How ya doing, Joon? You stay good, okay?" he'd say.

Every Saturday evening, the maître d' would bring the Steins, a handsome elderly couple in their eighties, to my table. Mrs. Stein always wore a beautiful dress complemented by sparkling jewelry. Dick dedicated a song, "I Have but One Heart," to the Steins, and they would dance. Watching them expressing their feelings of love to each other was beautiful.

One night, Mr. Stein glanced at me without saying a word as I was clearing tables. Then, as he left their table, he reached out and shook my hand. I felt something in my palm, a five-dollar bill. (That was when a loaf of bread cost twenty cents and a beer at the ballpark was eighteen cents.) I thought, perhaps, he saw himself, once young and poor, in me.

Putting in eight hours at the window factory, six hours bussing tables, and three hours driving between the two jobs, I had only seven hours each day to sleep, eat, and shower. Fatigue would eventually cause constant nosebleeds and a kind of vertigo that would make a bright blue sky turn yellow when I lifted my head to look up.

One day, I was in such a haze, I brushed my teeth with a popular hair cream, Brylcreem, famous for its contagious advertising jingle, "A little dab'll do ya." It came in a tube just like toothpaste. I could have done without that little dab, which I promptly spit into the sink in shock.

I was in such a fog I constantly risked accidents on the road. I would drive through red lights and make sudden wrong turns.

On one weekend, I went to bed on a Friday night in my attic apartment, which was nothing more than a small room with the bed a foot off the floor, a washbasin, a shower, and a toilet. The ceiling was not high enough for me to stand up straight. Chicago summers are hot and humid and there was no air conditioning and no fresh air.

I woke up at noon Sunday.

I could not believe my watch and clock when I realized what day it was. I had slept thirty-eight hours straight. When I got up, I was soaked in sweat. I had not set the alarm so I could sleep a few more hours on Saturday morning.

When I explained to the kitchen manager at the Congress what had caused me to miss my Saturday shift, he did not believe it at first. But listening to my story and seeing my honest expression, he took me at my word.

The savings from two jobs were not enough to cover two semesters' room and board and other miscellaneous expenses. The exchange-student assistance program provided tuition but nothing else. At the time, there was no student loan program. I knew I would need to take the 1963 school year off and work full-time to pay for the next two semesters.

I thought there had to be more ways to reach my goal in America. I knew I must be patient and re-energize before continuing to move on to success. I was undaunted and determined to continue my audacious pursuit of success, whatever path I chose.

CHAPTER THIRTEEN

Kyuhee

As I look back today on 1963, missing two semesters for not having enough money to go back to school motivated me to work harder to overcome the hardship. As usual, I worked nonstop at various jobs at a frenetic pace. I seemed to be on the move continuously.

I worked at the American Meat Slicing Machine Company, which sat in a row of similar shops on the west side of Chicago. Evenings, I had a regular shift as a dining room helper at a very popular Italian restaurant, Armando's, where you would hear diners and waiters speaking Italian as if they had just arrived from Rome.

Occasionally, I would notice well-known actors I had seen on TV. The Three Stooges would drop in, looking and acting just as they did in their TV shorts. Armando's typically served pasta and veal and chicken parmesan cooked in the wood-fired brick oven on thick ceramic plates.

Mr. Armando, the hands-on owner who looked just like the actor Joe Pesci, paid attention to everything going on in the dining room. He stood by the check-in counter, greeted his favorite customers, then table-hopped to chat with diners.

On Saturdays, the dining room was so crowded it was difficult for me to pass through the narrow hallway to the kitchen carrying a tray full of thick empty plates stacked like a pyramid. Mr. Armando would chase after me and pinch me on the hip for not cleaning the tables quickly enough.

The customers standing in the hallways by the bar, drinking martinis and smoking cigars, some kissing, would not make room for me to pass through to the kitchen. I had to yell, "Coming through, coming through with hot stuff," carrying an oval tray full of empty plates and glasses, weighing a ton, on my right shoulder supported by my right hand.

Still, after my various jobs, I had not saved enough to cover two semesters. I decided to skip one more semester.

That summer in Chicago, I met Kyuhee.

My sister-in-law, Charlene, who had watched me being so tired during the week, then sleeping all day Sundays, told me that two cute nurses from Korea arrived at the Wesley Memorial Hospital and suggested that I take one out on a date.

The following Sunday, I went to the hospital and told the receptionist I had come to see a nurse named Lee, who had recently arrived from Korea. The receptionist searched her Rolodex and said, "Oh, yes, we have two who arrived last week, both named Miss Lee. Which Lee would you like to see?"

I stood motionless because I forgot to ask Charlene their first names. Finally, the receptionist looked at the work schedule sheet. "One is working now. You can see the other Lee. I will have her come down to the lounge, so please wait there," she said.

The lounge looked like a library, with a high ceiling and walls lined with books. It was furnished with oversized chairs and long soft couches. I sat at the end of one sofa, so fluffy and soft that I sunk deeply, crossed my fingers, and waited hopefully.

The huge lounge door opened, and there appeared a pretty nurse in a white uniform. I was transfixed. My world suddenly stood still. I thought she was an angel sent by God.

I stood, frozen, not remembering what I had prepared to say. I introduced myself as the brother-in-law of Charlene Bai, a dietician at the hospital. She kept blinking her eyes and looking straight at me, not saying a word. She sat in a chair across from me.

I do not remember how long I spoke. It could have been thirty minutes or an hour. I told her about my school, my brother Ben, and my life since I came to America. She, finally, spoke about her work and how difficult it was to understand the accents of doctors when they ordered medication.

"I worry about making mistakes on doctor's orders," she said in concerned voice.

"I had the same experience when I first came to America," I replied.

"I could not understand a word the dean of students said about the school and dormitory when I first met him," I told her.

As I was leaving, I asked her if I could call her. She said yes and gave me her room phone number. Later, Kyuhee asked the nursing department to change her schedule to the morning shift.

The following Sunday evening, we went for a walk in Lincoln Park on Chicago's North Side under a bright moon. Before we ended our stroll, I heard two hearts pounding as I reached out to hold her hand.

The Sunday evening after that, we drove Lake Shore Drive and sat on a bench at Shedd Aquarium by Lake Michigan, gazing at the stars. She stopped talking and looked at the moon. I sensed she was missing her family.

Kyuhee told me her parents had five daughters and one son. Her father died of heart failure when she was a senior in high school. After his passing, her mother took over the trade business run by her father, which failed soon after.

In the Korean tradition, her family shared meals from pots on a knee-high table, around which everyone sat on a stone-covered floor. Her hungry sisters would devour nearly all the food on the table at every dinner, leaving just a few bites for Kyuhee.

Korean homes were heated ambiently by flues under the floor. Kyuhee would fall asleep on the warm floor under the table right after dinner, exhausted from working long hours with a half-empty stomach, before her mother woke her and sent her to bed.

She graduated from Yonsei University, the most prestigious University in Seoul, and worked at the University Hospital for two years. She then took a job offer from the American Nursing Association for graduate nurses at Wesley Memorial Hospital. The pay was much higher, and the opportunity to go to America was too attractive.

She arrived in San Francisco on May 1, 1963.

∽

That summer, I worked at the lithography department of the Continental Can Company on West Chicago Avenue.

To qualify for a high-paying job, an applicant had to be at least five feet ten inches tall and weigh 175 pounds. I was five feet six inches and weighed 120 pounds, but I was not deterred as I filled out the application. The salary was twice that offered for a part-time factory job and would help me immensely.

I filled out the application and watched in shock as the personnel manager tossed it into the trash. I pleaded with him that I could do the job and explained that I needed to save money to go back to school to continue my education. The personnel manager, with a big round belly and white mustache, waived the job qualification and hired me.

He risked his place in the company to find a way to help a young man he had just met.

The job I coveted was available because the regulars had gone to Florida for their summer vacation. That's where part-timers came in. The work was physically demanding. Four varnished printed plates, each larger than thirty inches by thirty inches with a combined weight of approximately ten pounds, were fed onto a conveyor belt that passed through a long, gas-fired oven to dry.

As the conveyor belt rolled by, wearing leather gloves for protection I grabbed the warm plates, lifted them off the belt, and stacked them on a wooden pallet with three corner guards.

If I removed one plate too slowly or dropped one, the remaining three would fall on the floor, causing a pileup and setting off an emergency stop to the entire line and probably ending my job. There were six conveyors, and the five other operators all seemed to me at least six feet tall and over two hundred pounds. They had worked the job for years, and it seemed they did it effortlessly.

The stacking table was built to stand to their height, making me put in extra effort to heave them up on the table. Just a few inches made it so much harder for me. The work was exhausting, but I never faltered.

I did not have time to wipe the sweat dripping down my face nor to watch the giant clock that hung on the wall for us to see when it was break time. I survived three months of hard work, driven by my determination to earn money to finish my education, and to honor the personnel manager who trusted that I could do the job.

As I left the plant on my last day, I walked by the personnel manager's office and bowed my head to thank him. He raised his thumb with a big smile.

Still, after my various jobs, I had not saved enough to cover two more semesters. I decided to skip one more semester, a total of three semesters, a year and a half on the academic calendar. It was a fortuitous break.

Kyuhee and I dated every Sunday, and our relationship had deepened. I began to feel Kyuhee was everything in the world to me. There was not a moment in the day I did not think of her. Every time I faced hardship, I thought of Kyuhee and saw her sweet smile encouraging me to stay on course and give my best. I wanted to live the rest of my life with someone I loved dearly.

I bought a ring with a tiny diamond from a downtown jeweler and took her out to the finest restaurant in Chicago, The Top of the Rock, on the forty-first floor of the Prudential Building on Michigan Avenue. It was September 7, 1963.

We sat at a corner table overlooking Lake Michigan and Grant Park. I knelt beside the table and proposed to Kyuhee. Tears welled in her eyes as she nodded and said, "Yes."

I was startled when I heard applause and several shouts of "Congratulations" from people near our table. As my pounding heart subsided, I looked at Kyuhee and said, "I am the happiest I have ever been."

After I kissed her goodnight and watched her walk into her hall, I drove to the lake. Under the moon, I knelt again and thanked God for giving me a life.

∽

I skipped yet another semester to continue to work, then transferred from the School of Mine & Metallurgy to the main campus of the University of Missouri School of Engineering in Columbia.

The university had a medical center and we hoped Kyuhee would find work there. I told Kyuhee as soon as I returned to school, I would help her to apply for a job there. After Continental Can that summer, I worked at a paint-mixing factory on North Kedzie Avenue in Chicago.

On November 22, 1963, a Friday, the news broke that President John F. Kennedy had been assassinated in Dallas. I was shocked and saddened by the death of such a charismatic man. I greatly respected him for his deep compassion for the disadvantaged of all colors and nationalities.

Kyuhee once told me that President Kennedy and I had two things in common, a gentle smile and a cowlick. I could not get my hair to sit down, the reason I had that tube of Brylcreem I tried to brush my teeth with.

We both prayed for President Kennedy to travel a peaceful journey from death to eternity, and we prayed that God embrace his beautiful wife, Jacqueline, their two children.

We lived together in a small apartment on Elain and Clark Street on the North Side for four months, preparing for my new semester at the new campus. I left Chicago in January 1964 for Columbia, and Kyuhee moved back to the resident hall at Wesley and remained in Chicago.

I kissed her goodbye and drove away on Chicago Avenue, watching her standing and waving in the rearview mirror.

It was a long, late-night drive to Columbia, but I did not feel tired driving and looking down the headlight beams on a dark Route 66, thinking of Kyuhee. We exchanged letters every day during a separation that winter and spring that was interrupted only by a few too-brief trips to Chicago on holiday weekends.

CHAPTER FOURTEEN

Love Letters

January 29, 1964

Dear Joon,

I was relieved to hear that you arrived at Columbia safe and well.

I felt sad when I knew our separation was imminent. After you left me, I cried for hours as if the world had left me. It was the first time in my life I experienced such sorrow of missing someone. I could not stop crying as I could see you appear in front of my eyes.

Thinking of you driving overnight without enough sleep worried me. I was shivering with the thought you left and would not be with me. I knelt and prayed that you would arrive at Columbia safely.

On that night, it hit me with the belief that you are the whole world to me. I could not sleep. I questioned if I could ever love you more than I love you now. I thanked God for creating a wonderful world.

Love you,
Kyuhee

February 1, 1964

Dear Joon,

Thinking about how difficult it would be to catch up with your study after a long absence from school made me empathize with you. You said our love for each other grows deeper through our separation. I believe the same.

I saw the most breathtaking view I have ever seen; a big, bright, orange-colored sun was rising over Lake Michigan during the shift change last night at around five in the morning. It was like the lake was on fire. I wished you were with me.

Living alone at the nursing residence for two years in Seoul, I experienced loneliness, but today, since you left me, I found out how lonely life can be. Loneliness is the soul's worst enemy, I thought. But seeing you in the picture and that bright sunshine lift the fog off the lake brings hope and keeps the loneliness away from me. So, I am not lonely anymore because I have you.

Today is Sunday, but I went down to the mailbox to see if your mail was in it. I walked to the lake and saw the pheasants peeking into the sand and chasing each other.

I sat on the bench and prayed to God to keep you safe and continue to bless me to love you with all my heart.

Love you,
Kyuhee

February 12, 1964

Dear Joon,

White powder snow dropped last night. So, this morning, it felt good to step on fresh snow, not melted and iced, and not have to dance to walk to the hospital.

Last night, it was a busy shift, many new patients were admitted, and some were discharged.

One of the patients, Mary, a nurse of thirty years at Wesley, who had been suffering from cancer, passed away. I was saddened. And the patient, John, who was close to death, lifted his hand to touch me.

I held a cold, wrinkled hand with just bones to give comfort until he got tired and went to sleep. I prayed to God to keep John in peace.

This morning, there was a foot of snow on Chicago Avenue. Two trucks passed by, one to remove snow and the other to spray salt. I wished it melts away before you come to see me.

Love you,
Kyuhee

April 3, 1964

Dear Joon,

Right after you left, it rained hard. I worried about where you would be, past Springfield? St. Louis? You drove eight hours in the rain to come to touch me and hold me in your arms. I once again felt your deep love for me.

To love you is a privilege and our understanding and sacrifice for each other are the basis of our true love.

The happiest time since you left was when I read your letters. Sometimes, I got impatient with the tightly glued envelope and tore it open to find the letter. Then, I read it three times, glancing at you in the picture on the table before putting it in the drawer.

Today, I went to the powder room during the break and looked at myself in the mirror. There, your face appeared, and I saw we looked very much alike. And I felt how blessed I am to have you standing by me, every minute of each wakening hour.

I thought about learning more about you, your character, desires, hopes, what you like, and what would make you happy. I want to know more about you, so I will become your wife.

I prayed the time speeds, so we see each other again soon. I prayed that you would graduate from school, become successful in your career, and be my proud husband.

Let us wait till that time with patience. Then, the strength of the bond holding us together will get us there.

Love you,
Kyuhee

April 16, 1964

Dear Joon,

I got up at around eight in the evening when you called. Working the night shift and frequent changes in the work shift made me tired. Some days I start the shift half-asleep and wake up by the time the shift ends. I was tired and thirsty when you called. I was not sure whether your call was in my dream or after I woke up.

I tried to piece together what we talked about and remembered that I forgot to tell you, "I love you." I immediately wanted to call you back, but one dollar per one-minute call was too expensive when I realized it was the exact cost for a one-day resident fee at Wesley. But to know that you are fine made me feel better. So, I went right back to sleep and had a dream.

In the dream, I met your parents in Seoul, there was a large house, both of your parents wore traditional Korean dress, your father in dignity, and your mother had a warm smile.

They said that they welcomed me to the Bai Family. We then went to the Tumen River to wash clothes, threw the pebbles into the river, and climbed the hill holding hands.

Then, we were the refugees in the war running away from the bombs. I tried to run with you, holding hands, but the mass of refugees pushed us and forced us to be separated.

I was looking for you everywhere, crying, but could not find you. Then, finally, I saw you, injured on your leg and helpless, in the battleground. You embraced me, and I was reaching out to touch your face.

I woke up, but my hand was still searching to touch you.

I missed you in my dream and the sound of your breathing when you slept next to me.

Joon, I miss you, and I love you.

Love,
Kyuhee

April 26, 1964

Dear Joon,

Just before the end of the night shift, my patient John was not in bed. So, I looked for him in the bathroom. There he was on the floor, already dead. Unfortunately, one assistant nurse was on vacation leave, so I had to call a male nurse from the other floor for his assistance to remove the body. I prayed that John's spirit is with God and with his loved ones.

Today is Sunday, so I went to the neighborhood church with Bo Hak Lee, the sixteenth-floor Korean nurse who came to Wesley the same week I did.

Going to church after a long absence, I felt like a lost sheep coming back to her home.

The sermon was 2 Corinthians: 12:9-10. "My grace is sufficient for you, for my power made perfect in weakness. Therefore, I will boast all the more gladly about my weakness so that Christ's power may rest on me. That is why, for Christ's sake, I delight in weakness, in insults, in hardships, in persecution, in difficulties. For when I am weak, then I am strong."

At the church, I prayed to God to bless me with three things: to give me abundant love to give to you, give filial piety to my mother and care for my siblings, and unwavering faith in God.

In the afternoon, friends at Wesley came, unannounced, and took Bo Hak and me to the cafeteria to treat me to ice cream and coffee. They all told me that I should get married before I leave for Columbia.

It has rained steadily since this morning, reminding me of the monsoon season in Korea.

The rest of the day, I thought about getting married to you.

It was a good Sunday.

Love you and miss you,
Kyuhee

CHAPTER FIFTEEN

The Wedding

We had no money for our wedding.

We reached out to the churches on the North Side to find one that would conduct the ceremony for us, but unfortunately, all of them replied that they conduct wedding ceremonies only for their congregants.

Then a light appeared unexpectedly. Reverend Alvern Erickson, the father-in-law of my good friend Don Chung, said he would perform the ceremony at his Portage Park Covenant Church on the west side of Chicago.

We had no money even for Kyuhee's wedding dress. We asked recently married friends if we could borrow a gown, but none would fit. Then a second light appeared unexpectedly. One of my high school classmates, Kim Dong Ho, who had married a few weeks earlier, offered his bride's dress, and luckily, it fit Kyuhee perfectly. Things were working out.

My brother Ben told us he would arrange a wedding reception at the church and an evening party at his apartment. Kyuhee had worn a borrowed gown and new white shoes. Oh, those white shoes!

She had forgotten to bring the new shoes to the church. I was in the groom's room a half-hour before the ceremony when Kyuhee's bridesmaid rushed in to tell me of the dilemma. I gave my car keys to my good friend Woo Hyung and asked him to rush the fourteen blocks to our apartment and retrieve the shoes.

My Ford Fairlane had a manual-shift transmission, and Woo Hyung did not know how to operate it. It took him an hour to return because he had stalled the car at every stoplight on the way to the apartment and back. By the time he returned, the stress had turned him as pale as a ghost, and he was drenched in sweat.

No one would have even noticed Kyuhee's shoes because her long gown covered them. It only delayed the wedding for thirty minutes. But I understood. Those shoes were the only new things she could wear at her wedding.

On September 2, 1964, Reverend Erickson solemnized our marriage.

We were married! I was the luckiest man in the world, and I thanked God for my union with the most beautiful girl in the world and the greatest gift I could receive, Kyuhee. A few of my close friends who attended colleges in the Chicago area came for an intimate reception at Ben's apartment.

I needed to be at school the next day to register for classes. So, after the party, we left for the long drive to Columbia in my old Fairlane, loaded with a trunk full of gifts, including three Chinese teapots.

It was almost midnight; sensing Kyuhee was tired, I decided we would rest for the night. I pulled over at a truck-stop motel, the Tropicana, on Route 66 on the outskirts of Chicago.

We checked in and quickly went down to the bar. There, we found a thick, smoke-filled room with two pool tables and truck drivers in cowboy boots, drinking. I was about to offer drinks to everyone in the bar, but Kyuhee quickly pushed me to the door.

We took two cans of Pabst Blue Ribbon beer to the room. The room smelled of gasoline, the bedsheets were stained with motor oil, and the bed offered a shaking massage, five minutes for ten cents.

We were exhausted from the long day of the excitement of getting married. We opened the canned beer, and I said to Kyuhee, "Cheers to my bride. I am sorry we could not drink champagne and dance to a band on our wedding day."

Kyuhee blinked her eyes just like she did when we first met in the lobby of the Wesley Memorial residence hall, and as she looked down at me when I proposed to her. She kissed me and said, "This is the happiest moment of my life. I am your wife."

It was a beautiful honeymoon for us. It could not be any better, I thought, because there were only two of us deeply in love. The unique environment was a novelty to both of us—a beautiful, adventurous way to start our lives as a married couple. We embraced those happy moments with joy, a gift of God.

CHAPTER SIXTEEN

Our New Lives Begin

Kyuhee and I became parents to our son James during my senior year.

It was not an easy time. Our precarious financial situation continued. Kyuhee's job at the university hospital was our income, and it was insufficient to support a comfortable life.

Take, for example, our 350-square-foot student apartment on the top floor of an old three-story Victorian building, for which we paid thirty-five dollars a month rent. The building had no elevator, and the stairs creaked as we climbed. We shared a bathroom with three other male tenants, all international students.

The bathroom certainly had seen better days. It had an old, metal claw-foot tub, the sort you'd see in old Westerns. Often, the boys left the tub uncleaned, so I had to clean it before we bathed.

The apartment was poorly lit, with two small windows, one in our tiny bedroom and another in the equally tiny kitchen that could accommodate only one person to stand and cook. A queen-size bed and a crib filled the bedroom. We had a small dining table with two chairs, a desk, and a small portable television in what passed for a living room and dining room.

James' birth was difficult. Kyuhee was in labor for forty-eight hours. I had two crucial final examinations coming up, so I studied by her bedside, holding her hand to comfort her. As Kyuhee's labor stretched into its second day, the doctor gave me the final say on whether Kyuhee should go through a Cesarean section. I asked the doctor to wait a few more hours.

James was a natural-born healthy baby, five pounds, ten ounces.

We placed James' crib in the corner of our cramped bedroom. Occasionally plaster from the ceiling fell on the crib, so I covered it with a blanket, creating a tent to keep James from getting hurt.

There were no disposable diapers at that time, and if there were, we could not afford them. I had to carry dirty diapers down four flights to a dark and damp basement to the apartment's rickety washing machine, so old it had a manual wringer and no hot-water connection.

I'd load the diapers, then try to study while I watched the machine shake through the cycles and sputter to a stop. Then I'd pull out the wet diapers and squeeze out the water by running them through the wringer by hand.

There was no dryer, so I would carry wet and heavy diapers upstairs to the ground floor and hang them on the wooden porch at the apartment entrance. The diapers became stiff as they dried in the sun, so I had to rub them with my hands to make them more pliable.

∽

The hard work, the cramped apartment, and the years of study became well worth the wait when I graduated with a bachelor of science degree in mechanical engineering in June 1966.

My sister Jung Sook came down to Columbia and attended the graduation ceremony. She sat proudly in the audience next to Kyuhee, holding baby James.

It was an emotional occasion for us, knowing we had overcome significant obstacles to reach that day. "We did it. Now we can start our new life at our second home, Chicago," I told Kyuhee as I gripped my diploma gratefully.

Earlier, I had interviewed for a job with Bill Hodgson, technical director of the Extrudo Film Company—a subsidiary of Standard Oil, in Lake Zurich, Illinois, a suburb of Chicago—who came to the school to recruit a process engineer.

Bill chose me.

CHAPTER SEVENTEEN

New Job, New House

We packed our belongings into the beat-up Ford Fairlane and drove to Rolling Meadows, a small town twenty-five miles northwest of Chicago, close to Lake Zurich.

Just as we arrived at the motel, we heard the wailing of a tornado siren and watched, awed, as strong winds snapped nearby tree branches. The strange noises and commotion frightened baby James, who began crying. Soon the tornado passed, taking with it our worries.

I joined a team that developed a new film to create a moisture barrier that would make disposable diapers like Pampers and Kimbies, which brought substantial commercial success to the company. Within a year, I was promoted to oversee the quality assurance programs at the three Extrudo manufacturing plants, in Lake Zurich, Pottsville, Pennsylvania, and Wentzville, Missouri.

My rise in the company arrived at the same time as a real estate development boom in the towns surrounding Chicago's O'Hare International Airport that offered affordable down payments and low-interest rates on new houses.

I asked my boss, the general manager, John De Manuel, for a loan of five thousand dollars to deposit toward the purchase of the

1,800-square-foot house in Elk Grove that was selling for sixteen thousand dollars. John wrote the check and said, "No interest. However, I would like you to pay it back in twelve months."

We became homeowners. Exhilarated, I thought of my family in Korea.

After two years, Extrudo sponsored me for US citizenship. Soon after, I sponsored my sister Jung Sook, who would come to America to stay with us while she attended college in Joliet. She met a young Korean student, Hwang Byung-Soo, and Kyuhee and I arranged for their wedding.

I had also invited my younger brother Ken and his wife, Ok-Nam. Ken began to work at Extrudo as an operator and lived with Ok-Nam in a small apartment in Lake Zurich.

Kyuhee and I welcomed our second son, Stephen, a healthy baby boy who was an easy delivery at the same hospital where she worked, St. Alexis, three blocks from our new house.

My new assignment called for much travel. Driving to the Sky Top Lodge in Pennsylvania's Poconos to attend a national sales meeting, I saw a rugged mountain landscape that reminded me of my hometown in Korea. I was told the movie *The Deer Hunter* was filmed in the area.

Even then, so early in my career, I dreamed of the future. "If I ever build a factory of my own someday, it would be in the Poconos," I *promised* myself.

In 1972, I was recruited by the Northern Petrochemical Company (Norchem), which was looking for highly qualified polymer engineers. Norchem had recently built a large facility in the middle of a cornfield in Morris, Illinois, to manufacture polyethylene and polypropylene resins used to make products like packaging film, trash bags, construction film, and agricultural film.

I was torn. On one hand, I was indebted and loyal to Extrudo, which had recruited me from college, sponsored me to become a citizen, helped me purchase a new house, and had promoted me rapidly to a high-level position. On the other hand, the Norchem job had enormous growth potential.

And if that was not complicated enough, at the same time I heard that I was being considered for a section manager position at Extrudo's parent company, Humble Oil, at its refineries in Bayonne, New Jersey, a big promotion. The Norchem job offered different advancement opportunities for my career, and the chance to remain in the Chicago area.

Over breakfast, I told Kyuhee about the Norchem opportunity in Joliet. Although the distance from Elk Grove was only fifty miles, Norchem assisted relocation. The move would mean the end of her job at St. Alexis, a wonderful convenience for the mother of two young children. Kyuhee paused and looked at me.

"I trust that you have given it serious consideration, and I appreciate you for asking for my opinion. I know that you always think about the best interests of our children and me. I am and will always be with you and appreciate your decision," she said.

I took the Norchem job, which called for me to oversee its quality control activities that tested and assured that finished products met specifications. Soon after, the technical center director, Dr. Ed Fettes, promoted me to application group manager, with responsibilities that included internal product development and customer support. I would soon be traveling all over the country, showing customers' workers how to develop new items and improve production.

In 1974, Dr. Fettes asked me if I could give technical assistance, as a loan assignment, to one of our affiliates, National Poly Product Company in Mankato, Minnesota, on their cast film processing.

The assignment was for four months, from November through February, the coldest time of the year in that northern city. Every Monday, I left home in Joliet in the early morning to catch a 7:00 a.m. flight from Midway Airport to Minneapolis-St. Paul Airport, rent a car, drive another hour and a half to Mankato, and arrive at the plant at around ten.

I made one mistake. I wrote a note on the blackboard of the plant supervisor's office with my room phone number at the Holiday Inn saying that workers could call me if there was a problem.

It was so cold I had to cover the hood of my Chevy rental car with an electric blanket every evening before I checked in.

Every morning at around 1:00 or 2:00 a.m., the technicians called me with various problems. I'd go out in the frigid air and start the car to let it warm up, then drive to the plant over icy Mankato streets feeling as if the car and I were waltzing, watching the hanging streetlights sway in the normal, early morning high winds. There were no cars on the street at that hour, thank God.

Once I made it safely to the plant, I worked on the huge casting machine under bright lights accompanied by the noise of the heavy machinery. A coffee break offered me the joy of sharing time with technicians and supervisors talking about Bears versus Viking's football games. Finally, I danced the waltz back to the hotel to catch a few hours of sleep. I was dead tired. Nevertheless, I felt satisfied knowing that I had done my best for the company.

Every late Friday afternoon, going back home, I stopped by a discount toy store near the airport to bring home toys for my boys.

CHAPTER EIGHTEEN

New Horizons in Sales

I began to enjoy my new job, particularly visiting clients to provide technical support and solutions to problems. For me, these visits were a chance to roll up my sleeves and help to promote our product, which I became very good at.

On one occasion, I called on Rubbermaid in Winchester, Virginia, to provide technical assistance in processing Norchem resins. I stayed through midnight, working with shift operators. As I left the factory early the following day, plant managers were pleased with the results and expressed their appreciation. I was tired and hungry but happy and satisfied I could help.

On another trip, a long scorching summer day at a plant in Elsa, Texas, I demonstrated a new cast film process. I dug right in, showing, not telling, the process know-how with my hands covered in grease as I sweated profusely. The operators saw that and appreciated my hands-on teaching approach. By the time I left the plant, they were processing at a 30 percent higher rate with nearly zero waste.

I enjoyed the day and felt good for bringing about such dramatic results. I began to realize my strength was delivering technical service to my customers, many of whom wrote and called Bob Patten, national sales manager, and Stu MacEachern, V.P. of sales and marketing, to express their appreciation for my work.

I even received praises for a technical article I wrote, "The Impact of Color Concentrates on P.E. Film Property," published in the company newsletter.

I was happy to see my contributions to my customers were well received and appreciated. So much so that I asked Stu to transfer me to the sales group. He enthusiastically agreed, saying he had been considering offering me a place in his sales force.

Joining the sales group was the best thing that happened to my professional career.

My first sales assignment was to call on accounts in the midwestern district, which covered the Chicago area and Indiana, Michigan, and Wisconsin. I enjoyed driving and visiting small towns like Sheboygan Falls, Appleton, Green Bay, Grand Rapids, and large cities like Milwaukee, Detroit, Gary.

For my customers, the raw material made up close to 75 percent of the cost of finished products they manufacture. The people I called on ranged from owners of small and midsize companies to presidents of large companies.

On one trip to Wisconsin, I stopped to make a phone call at a roadside public phone booth. I asked the operator for the phone number of the hotel near Sheboygan Falls Plastics, which I was calling on. For some reason, perhaps my accent, the operator asked me where I was from.

I told her that I had arrived from Paris, France last night. From her voice on the other side, I could hear that she was intrigued by the exotic traveler on the other end of the call. She kept asking personal questions.

"Are you traveling with your wife?"

"Is it your first time in America?"

I had to apologize to her for ending the conversation by saying I was on a tight schedule. I also thought it was good to hang up because I had to drop another quarter into the phone to continue our conversation.

Later, as I sat with the company owner, Bill, I noticed he was not looking at my face and appeared uncomfortable. I had not seen a single Asian face while driving in that part of the country, and I figured the owner had not either. I thought I needed to break the ice. I told him about my conversation with the operator an hour before and how she had been intrigued by my accent.

To my surprise, he suddenly laughed out loud, saying, "That's funny." Then he asked me about my past and where I was staying. He later invited me to the town's famous barbeque place, where we had a terrific dinner of pulled pork and ribs. We had a fantastic time drinking and chatting late into the night.

I soon fell into a very comfortable routine.

Every Friday, I stopped by my office in Des Plaines on Chicago's northwest side to write my call report, see the guys from the other territories, and compare notes. On summer Fridays, I'd occasionally have a chance to go to a Chicago Cubs game at Wrigley Field, located close to the office, where I loved sitting in the right-field bleacher section above the storied ballpark's ivy walls drinking eighteen-cent Hamm's beer. I became a rabid Cubs fan.

The bleachers at Wrigley Field were always raucous. Every time the opposing right fielder took his position, the Bleacher Bums exchanged good-natured trash talk with him. We hollered at him, "Hey, Jose, you look clean today. Who did you sleep with last night?"

In those days, the Cubs had a team of iconic players, the best around, but they never seemed to do well enough to make it to the division championship game. I watched Ernie Banks, a future Hall of Fame shortstop, take the field with his teammate Ron Santo, a third baseman and another future Hall of Famer.

Always affable Ernie Banks was known as "Mr. Cub." I enjoyed watching him hit home runs with his sweet swing and run the bases flashing a boyish grin.

Wrigley Field at the time had no lights, and the Cubs played all their games during the day and played more doubleheaders than other teams. Ernie Banks became famous for his signature expression, "Let's play two today."

We would all stand during the seventh inning stretch and sing along with television announcer Harry Caray, who'd lean from his booth above home plate and lead the crowd of thirty thousand plus in singing "Take Me Out to the Ballgame." I sang as loud as I could, "One, two, three strikes, you're out at the old ball game . . ." Then we all yelled, "Hey, hey," clapping, jumping, and shaking the stands.

The highlight of any Cubs win was watching Ron Santo jump up and kick both heels together as he left the field after a winning game, which always prompted the Bleacher Bums to shout, "We won, we won."

There were not many wins those years for the Cubs, but it was an adorable team, tenacious.

The Cubs were my kind of team and will always be.

CHAPTER NINETEEN

Fuzzy

Life for me was much more than work.

Work was challenging, I thrived on challenges, and I enjoyed the benefits my hard work provided. But, as much as I loved work and its many challenges, Kyuhee and our sons meant more to me than anything. They were the essence of life itself, the true meaning of love for me, and the four of us shared many adventures.

In 1978, while I was with Norchem, I ran a quality-control lab in rural Morris, Illinois, beside a cornfield off the heavily traveled Route 66. It seemed, sadly to me, that people leaving Chicago, cars packed with children and belongings, would often stop by the roadside and abandon family pets. It happened more frequently than one would imagine. The dogs would wander around the vast cornfield for days and show up at my lab looking for food and water.

One dog snuck into the lab during a hot summer day when workers left an overhead door open to keep the lab cool. I discovered the dog hiding in a corner after all the technicians had gone home for the day. I stood over the dog wondering what to do. I could not just take him back out into the cornfield. I decided to take him home.

Before bringing him into the house, I called a veterinarian who had an office next to his house. Then I took the dog for rabies shots.

James and Steve, eight and six years old at the time, were excited to see the new addition to our family.

The poor dog's coat was a jumble of prickly goathead stickers and tumbleweeds from his days wandering outside, and I struggled to keep the boys from hugging him until we cleaned him up.

I had to use thick shop gloves to keep my hands safe from the goathead stickers. Then we all washed him in the tub in warm water and shampoo.

Finally, I lifted him from the tub, feeling his jutting ribs from his ordeal in the cornfield. After massaging him and brushing his freshly washed coat, we fed him with leftover soft food and warm milk. After he finished eating, the dog was tired and weak, barely awake, so he dropped by the tub and slept.

The next day, I bought a large bag of dog food, a collar, brushes, a leash, and dog biscuits from K-Mart. After two days with the dog, Stephen's eyes became puffy and red. Then, despite a prescription and treatment from an allergist, his puffy eyes got worse. Our new friend had to go. I took him to the local Humane Society to be adopted, left a donation and the things I bought at K-Mart, and dropped him off.

A month later, another dog, a big one this time, came into the lab. In heavy rain, I brought him to the same veterinarian, struggling to carry him, using my feet to open the door to the vet's office. After his shots, I brought him home to the boys. We repeated our cleaning regimen in the tub, slightly more difficult because of the dog's size.

Steve's puffy eyes returned, and two days later, I returned to the Humane Society. The person at the desk could not believe I was back again. He said, "Mr. Bai, you must love dogs."

The following summer, on a hot and humid day, I glanced up from my work at the lab and saw a small dog with black spots sprinkled on her fluffy white coat walking timidly toward me. I repeated my ritual at home, and to everyone's great and lasting relief, Steve had no allergic reaction. The boys named her Fuzzy.

Both James and Steve quickly fell in love with Fuzzy and rushed home from school each day to play with her, their new best friend.

Fuzzy sparked so much love and affection. Our family looked every day at her as a gift. She would later surprise us and give us some gifts of her own.

We went to Hawaii for a one-week vacation and left Fuzzy with my brother Ken, who lived in a large apartment complex near O'Hare airport. After our vacation, we stopped to pick up Fuzzy before heading home. When I opened the door to apartment building, still over one hundred feet from Ken's room, we heard Fuzzy barking.

When Ken opened the door, Fuzzy burst out, jumping gleefully on Kyuhee and me and the boys. When we calmed her down and walked into the family room, we were greeted with quite a surprise.

It seemed that two days before, Fuzzy had given birth to four puppies—on Ken's living room couch of all places, not exactly the best place to do so. I thanked Ken and paid to have the couch cleaned.

The boys loved Fuzzy's new puppies. They would later cry each time I gave a puppy away to a neighbor, but I had no choice.

I noticed something else during our puppy adventure, something that showed Kyuhee's loving nature. With all the disruptions the new puppies brought into our lives, Kyuhee supported us all the way. I saw very quickly that she was as excited as the boys. We all loved our Fuzzy.

Kyuhee and the boys enjoyed travel as much as I did. As summer approached one year, we came up with an idea to see as much of the country as we could. We called it our "See the USA" vacation, and we set out enthusiastically on a three-week road trip to see and educate ourselves about our country before we toured the rest of the world.

I bought a big Oldsmobile Custom Cruiser station wagon. The four of us set out, Kyuhee by my side and the boys in the back with back seats down, on an epic drive through the Midwest, the South, up the East Coast, to New York City, then back through the Northeast for a chance to see Niagara Falls near Buffalo, and finally back to home to Joliet.

We stopped in Florida, Washington DC, and Cape Cod. We saw the Kennedy Space Center, Sea World, Cocoa Beach, and Jacksonville, the monuments in Washington DC, the exuberant sights of New York City.

We gobbled down regional foods like lobster on Cape Cod, and we caught the wonders of the colorful Northeast landscape as we headed home.

CHAPTER TWENTY

Mastering the Art of Selling

My hard work in the field, my hands-on approach, and the positive results I produced, quickly caught the attention of Stu MacEachern, Norchem's vice-president of sales and marketing, who would promote me to district manager of the Midwest. That was only the beginning of a meteoric rise.

Three years into the Midwest job, the West Coast district sales manager Bill Doucette resigned, and I was asked to serve that district as well. I covered both districts for six months, staying for two weeks in Los Angeles to call on West Coast customers and two weeks at home to call on Midwest accounts. Norchem produced over 850 million pounds of resins annually, sold and serviced by fourteen field salesmen.

I sold 250 million pounds to thirty accounts in sixteen states in the two territories. Finally, after three months of traveling to two districts, Stu gave me a break. He promoted me to manager of the Western region, one of four regions in the country.

We moved to Mission Viejo, California, a small city about fifty miles southeast of Los Angeles. The Western region included eleven states and five major competitors, DuPont, Dow, Exxon, Union Carbide, USI, and Chemplex, each with a full sales staff. I loved the travel, meeting people, and the new experiences, though it pained me to be away from Kyuhee and two young sons.

During those years traveling as a field salesman, I had opportunities to see many parts of the country and met people in each state with its unique culture. I'd soon experience much more of America and its beauty and stunning variety.

I developed a special fondness for a company in Yakima, Washington, The Shield Bag and Print, and I looked forward to calling on them. I'd fly to Seattle, then chose to drive through White and Chinook passes in Mount Rainier on the way to Yakima, rather than hop on another quick flight.

I would always stop to rest near a stream halfway to the top of the mountain, where the stillness and breathtaking beauty were nothing short of magnificent. Whenever I came to that spot, I felt close to God, and I prayed and thanked God for all I was blessed with.

In winter, I'd often think about stopping at one of many ski slopes on my way to Yakima, but I never did. From Yakima, I would drive to another client in Portland, Oregon, down Routes 97 and 84 along the Columbia River, allowing myself to drink in even more pleasant scenery.

On a loan assignment, I traveled to Savannah, Georgia, to call on Georgia Pacific Paper. The special work request was to improve the laminating process with linear low-density resin on milk carton paper. I could smell the distinctive odor of paper pulp as soon as I stepped from the plane.

On my drive to the plant, I passed the plantation houses of another era. After my call, I had my first Southern-fried meal, catfish, at the famous Pirates restaurant with a local salesman.

My efforts continued to pay off. As a result, I was named Employee of the Year of Northern Natural Gas, the parent company of Norchem, two years in a row, an honor and distinction made more meaningful to me considering that it had sixty thousand employees.

The award was a Caribbean cruise with Kyuhee, but we opted to cash out for five thousand dollars and use the money to install drapes and window curtains at our new house in Mission Viejo.

My sales prowess caught the attention of one of my customers, Harry Engh, founder and owner of North American Plastics in Aurora, Illinois, who would ask each time I called on him if I would consider partnering with him on a western initiative he had long been considering.

"If I ever expand to the West Coast, I would only do so if you joined me," he told me. His offer was 20 percent ownership, a credit line, and complete authority to manage the company as vice president and general manager.

In 1978, I accepted Harry's offer, left Norchem, and created a new company, North America Plastics of California.

I moved to get into production as quickly as possible. In short order, I secured a ten thousand square-foot warehouse space in Tustin, about thirty-five miles southwest from Los Angeles, purchased two extruders and three bag-converting machines, and recruited eighteen employees.

We started three shifts working seven days a week. As general manager, I continued traveling, making sales calls to West Coast cities, in addition to managing the plant's daily operations—maintenance, shipping, receiving, accounting, and personnel. As a result, I had no time to rest.

Hard work by everyone in my group paid off. We brought the company to $1 million in sales the first year. After that, the company sales grew exponentially to $20 million, and generated over $2 million in profits the fifth year of operation in 1982.

Those were very productive and happy years for my family and me. While I was busy with the new company, Kyuhee worked at the Saddleback Community Hospital and our sons attended El Toro Middle School. We were a living embodiment of the American Dream.

Despite being busy with work and caring for our sons, Kyuhee attended to a long-held dream of doing missionary work. She took two weeks off to take a Christian missionary class.

In 1979, she earned certification from Los Angeles Missionary Bible Institute. She began visiting many Korean families in Mission Viejo and its surrounding towns to deliver her message of Christianity. I was impressed by her dedication.

Finally, we decided to fulfill and another long-held dream, bringing my mother to live with us. I had not seen my mother since I waved goodbye to her as she stood tearfully at the side of the runway in Yeouido Airport, Seoul, in 1959, twenty years before.

I wanted my mother to live with us and share the happiness.

CHAPTER TWENTY-ONE

Mother

Mother was a faithful, loving Christian who cared deeply for others, so much so she had made it a lifelong commitment. Her compassion colored everything she did.

She wanted to come to America to be with her loved ones. Her dream was to live with us in California and visit her three other sons and her daughter, all married, two living in Chicago, and two in New York.

She knew she would have to learn English and adjust to different culture and surroundings. She was certainly up for the challenge and not intimidated. She was bolstered by her endearing hope that she could work as an evangelist in Korean-American churches.

Before she came to the United States, I went to Seoul to accompany her on a round of farewell visits to Jung Neun Presbyterian church and its several Christian groups she had been a member of for decades. She also wanted to say goodbye, individually, to the team of women evangelists she recruited and taught decades ago.

I witnessed more than a thousand congregants gather at the church to pray for my mother and bid her farewell, many embracing her in tears. Some pled with her to not leave them. I wondered what she had done to be loved by so many people, so profoundly.

From the moment my mother joined us in California, our home became a healthier place. Mother was a prayer and a healer for her grandsons. Whenever one of the boys caught a cold or was sick, her prayers made them healthy again.

She grew happy at the Korean church in Los Angeles, over an hour's drive from our house in Mission Viejo, and she enjoyed learning English and American ways.

She studied American history for months to prepare for the US citizenship test. She remembered the names of the first five and most recent five presidents of the United States, and of course, the sixteenth. I waited outside the immigration office for my mother to complete the test.

She emerged with a big smile, a confident smile, a US citizen smile. She passed the test with flying colors on her first try.

⟳

One summer, we took Mother to Yosemite National Park in the stunning high Sierras of Northern California. It was an adventurous trip that left me with fond and endearing memories.

We stayed for three days at the main campground lodge before venturing farther north for two more days at White Wolf Camp, where I filled the camp stove in our large tent with wood and stoked a fire to keep us warm in the morning chill in the high mountains.

When we reached the second camp, the boys asked for a smaller, separate tent.

It seems their grandmother's snoring had kept them awake. We rented two tents. Thinking my mother would be more comfortable, I let her sleep alone in the smaller tent while the rest of us took over a larger tent. It was a mistake.

I was startled awake by my mother's scream in the middle of the night. "Help! Save me, save me."

I rushed to her tent and found the side of her tent was scratched and partially torn open. Mother was shaking and clinging to me tightly. A bear had visited.

I filled the stove with wood and slept the rest of the night in her tent.

The following day as we walked down the valley, Mother gathered us under a thicket of majestic giant Sequoias and prayed for us. She was impressed with the view of the magnificent landscape, El Capitan, Bridal Falls, Half Dome, Glacier Point, and other majestic wonders in the valley. She prayed to God in thanks for the gifts of nature and healthy bodies and souls for our family.

～

Mother maintained her independence and strength. With Kyuhee working at the hospital, the boys attending school, and me either traveling or coming home late from work every night, she felt alone. She told me that she wanted to move to Koreatown in Los Angeles to be close to the Korean churches and other folks her age.

I moved her to an apartment for seniors in Koreatown, where, as usual, she settled in quickly, making friends with everyone. Every weekend, I would visit her to buy her groceries, take her to her favorite restaurants, and attend Sunday church services.

She stayed true to her Christian values wherever she lived.

Once, a delivery van struck Mother on the narrow street outside her apartment in Koreatown. She was thrown to the road by the force of impact, which tore her watch from her wrist and sent it several feet away. The shaken driver came to help Mother, who was in obvious pain, with bruises on her legs and forearms forming quickly.

She asked the driver if he went to church. The young man replied that he recently arrived from Korea and that he was not a Christian. Mother said to him, "If you promise me that you will attend church this Sunday, I will let you go." She did not call the police.

During the gas crisis in 1979, with shortages and long lines at service stations everywhere, I took the bus to Koreatown to attend a Christmas play presented by seniors at mother's church. She played the role of Cinderella's stepmother in the play.

I sat in the front row and heard her whisper the lines to other actors when they missed their cues. I wasn't surprised. She had an astounding memory. I remember Mother reciting the Gospel of Matthew chapter 5 verses 1–12 without holding a Bible.

She received the loudest applause when the play ended. I was so very proud of her.

Afterward, I took her to her favorite Naem Myung restaurant. On the long drive home, I thought how blessed I was to have such a presence in my mother.

CHAPTER TWENTY-TWO

A Time for Independence and Sorrow

After five years running North America Plastics of California, I decided to establish my own company.

I founded Trans Western Polymers in 1983 in Hayward, a San Francisco Bay-area city, and we moved the family to nearby Danville. I fulfilled my agreement with Harry, and we parted amicably.

Though Mother would join us later, we stopped by her apartment in Koreatown on our way up to Danville to say farewell. She stood by the car with tears running down her cheeks. All four of us in the car cried. As we pulled away, she continued waving at us until we could no longer see her.

We brought my mother to Danville soon after settling in our new home, and we started to attend a Concord Korean Baptist Church in Martinez with over five hundred congregants. As usual, Mother quickly made many friends at the church and became a senior Bible study group leader. In addition, Kyuhee became the director of a choir of fifty.

We would soon find ourselves in Korea for a joyous occasion. The Sejong Center for the Performing Arts in Seoul, a large theater with a capacity of three thousand, held an annual Christian choir competition during the holidays. Our church was selected from hundreds of Korean American churches across the country. Our choir flew to Seoul in 1992 and joined the competition.

The competition was intense. Twelve groups represented the prominent churches in Seoul, many with a congregation of more than ten thousand. The competing choirs had more than two hundred members each and were accompanied by bands. Some had orchestras.

Our choir of thirty-eight members, the only one from outside Korea, dressed in white with green bow ties and wide, decorative, matching belts and sang their hearts out. We won first prize.

Kyuhee, the winning choir director, was given a bouquet as the entire audience stood and applauded thunderously.

At the end of the contest, every choir member, more than a thousand strong, came out on stage, filling every possible open space. Some stood behind the curtain, others squeezed in where they could. And our music director, Dr. Min Ki Man, led the entire assembly in singing Handel's magnificent "Hallelujah Chorus." It was a breathtaking finale.

The competition ended gloriously with the sound of praising God that shook the city of ten million that night. I was so proud of Kyuhee, her team, and the country we represented, America. I felt Mother's prayers were with us.

On our flight back home, Kuhee and I spoke about how much we missed our mother, how much she would have enjoyed it if she had traveled with us.

∽

Our blissful existence continued uninterrupted until Mother fell and broke her right hip. Doctors at the Pittsburg Health Center implanted a metal plate to secure her broken bones.

She stayed at the hospital, a two-hour drive from my office, for six weeks, recuperating. Every night, I drove straight to her bedside after work, and we chatted until she took her medication and went to sleep. On Sundays, I pushed her in a wheelchair around a nearby park to breathe in the invigorating fresh air deeply and have a chance to see and smell the bright garden flowers.

Two weeks after I brought her home from the hospital, she fell and broke her left hip, which required another plate, and another six weeks in the hospital. It was a heartbreaking disappointment for us, and it was painful for me to think of her going through the process again.

Again, Mother's infinite grace showed through. Seeing me in agony, she tried to comfort me. It was a touching gesture, so true to her nature.

By the time I would arrive at the hospital, Mother had already eaten her dinner. I would sit by her bedside, and we would talk and reminisce. She'd discuss her day and rehabbing, and I would update her on family and world news.

In one bittersweet conversation, we spoke one evening about our peaceful times living in Haeryong before the war and our resilience moving to Busan in excruciating circumstances.

We talked about surviving in cold Busan and enduring the difficult times in Seoul when my father's business failed. We shed tears sharing the memories, but we always ended our conversation on an upbeat note, for Mother was an eternally optimistic woman.

When I left her bed, Mother often said, "Those were the happy times. We only had a love for each other." I treasured that time with my mother as she recovered, just the two of us in the hospital. It allowed me to express my love to her.

෴

I sensed she missed Father. He came to the United States once and stayed with us for a month in late 1970, then traveled to visit his sons and daughter in New York, New Jersey, and Chicago. We all gave Father the warm treatment. I took him to Disneyland, Sea World, and many attractions. My siblings gave him tours of the best places to see in New York City and Chicago.

It was not enough to entice him to stay.

My father was a stubborn and unyielding man. He refused to move to America to live with us under any circumstance. Before he returned to Seoul, he turned to me.

"I do not wish to come to America where I cannot converse, have no friends, and have nothing to do. Boredom will kill me," he said.

∽

During her stays in the hospital, Mother had kept a Bible on the lamp table next to her bedside and would pray for hours. Her faith in God gave her the strength to endure three months at the hospital and overcome physical pain and loneliness. She would often ask, "Joon, why is it? Why is life so short?"

She wanted to go back to Seoul to her daughter and to the church where she had served as a deacon for forty years. It was her spiritual home.

I flew to Seoul with her in the first-class cabin in September 1988, a glorious return made her happy but, during the flight, she cried about leaving Kyuhee and boys. Mother lived her last two years with my sister, Chung Sook.

She did not use her time for quiet contemplation. Instead, she practiced her Christian values of love and charity to their fullest. After returning to Seoul, she adopted a teenage girl, an orphan, named her Kyung Sook, our family name, and loved her just like her other children.

One afternoon, a traveling merchant truck that sells all kinds of goods, dresses, cloth, and general merchandise, common in Seoul, pulled into the apartment complex's parking lot. I had given Mother money to buy something for herself, a sweater and an overcoat for the coming winter, and some moisture creams. She picked out one sweater and opened her handbag to pay. Her wallet was missing. Someone had stolen it.

Mother did not become angry, nor did she call the police. Instead, she sat on a bench at the edge of the parking lot and prayed for the soul of the thief who had stolen her wallet. She later told my sister that if anyone needed money so badly that he had to steal from her, that man should have the money. That was my mother.

She died of heart failure on March 11, 1990.

At her funeral service, all three congregations at her church mourned, and a combined choir of more than four hundred sang her favorite hymns for hours: "Jesus Loves Me, This I Know"; "I Hear Thy Welcome Voice"; "God Be with You Untill We Meet Again," among many others.

Mother's resting place sits upon a hill near the outskirts of Seoul, facing north toward her beloved hometown of Haeryong, hundreds of miles away but so close to her heart.

Kyuhee held my hands, and we stood by Mother and looked north through our tears.

The epitaph on the headstone reads: Lee Yun Hee (Mother's maiden name) was the

Hero of Faith
Leader of Prayer
Warrior Evangelist

Later, on my many trips to Seoul, after stops in China and North Korea, I visited Mother. I missed only twice in nearly one hundred stopovers in Seoul, both times because of sudden weather changes; heavy rain made it too slippery and impossible to climb the hill.

I would bring fresh flowers and chat with her about the family, my work in North Korea, and her favorite Bible verses in Matthew's Gospel, just as we had done when she was recuperating at the hospital in Pittsburg.

My mother loved everyone she had met. She had kept me warm in the winter cold during our journey to Busan. She sent me to America. She had encouraged me and prayed for me to succeed in my efforts to help in North Korea and taught me how to express true love artistically through my film.

Above all, she taught me the meaning of love.

In front of her grave, I *promised* her that I would follow her prayers and spread her request to love others. She was and is God's daughter.

My mother always stays in my heart.

CHAPTER TWENTY-THREE

Trans Western Polymers

My early days in 1983 with my new company Trans Western Polymers were tense.

But I understood my industry and how it worked, and I was self-assured about my ability to run a company. After all, I had been very successful on my path to get to the point where I knew I wanted to be, owning a company of my own.

I also knew that there is no safety net when you step into a competitive world as the new kid on the block. My confidence came from my experience, where I learned that hard work would prevail.

Without any outside credit backing, starting a new company from scratch was entirely new territory for me. I found myself in a position I knew was inevitable. I understood clearly that I would have to take many chances, stretch myself thin financially, and hope and pray that everything would fall into place.

I knew I was compromising the future education of our two boys and the financial security of my family. Kyuhee's faith in God and trust in my audacity never wavered as we pulled up stakes in Southern California and moved our family north to Hayward to start a new chapter in our lives.

I chose Hayward, bay area, after I left my partnership with Harry because I did not want to create a conflict or take business away from him in Southern California. My reputation in the industry and the trust it engendered helped me establish credit lines with banks and suppliers.

I used a loan from the Small Business Administration, funds from the transfer of my shares back to Harry, and every dollar in my savings to purchase the two extruders and bag machines essential to begin operations.

It takes time to find new customers, primarily because potential customers have already committed to their suppliers for their private-label products. I made many sales calls with my new sales broker, Phil Sugg, but we could not secure any orders.

I decided to call on the director of the private label of The Market Wholesale, a distributor in Santa Rosa, California, by myself. I stayed up all night, sleepless, then drove to the Santa Rosa corporate office, arriving well before it opened. Waiting in the parking lot, I spotted an important-looking older man I felt could be the owner arriving at the office.

I followed him to the reception area, where I asked a woman at the desk if I could see the company owner. I told her I did not have an appointment when she asked. She went to the owner's office and came out and said to me that he would see me.

He was drinking coffee as I sat in a small chair in front of him, nervously waiting to start my sales pitch.

As I began to introduce myself, my company, and my product, I burst into tears. The owner, Don Meacham, was startled to see me crying. After hearing my story of how I started Trans Western Polymers and why I came to see him, he walked to me and lifted me from my chair, and said, "Joon, no need to cry. I will give you the business."

Don directed Harry Markowitz, the private-label product manager, to issue Trans Western Polymers' first order, a truckload of assorted items, for its Home and Garden label. In doing so he took business away from Presto Products, a prominent national supplier.

From that day, my faith in God grew more profound.

Why did Mr. Meacham agree to see me, someone he had not met, that morning? Why did he give me his business? The questions lingered.

It was God's blessing, I believed.

CHAPTER TWENTY-FOUR

Growth, Wonderful Growth

As Trans Western Polymers got off the ground and I began to breathe a bit easier, I drew strength from three things and used them to sustain me when things became tense. Starting a new company had its inherent tensions, of course.

First, I had the love and support of Kyuhee. Second, together we had our undiluted faith in God. Third, I summoned in rare moments of doubt the fact that I knew the bags made at my factory were the best in the world. I needed only to get the word out.

I would use my thumb test of stretching, puncturing, and tearing bags, and I found no bags out-tested mine, no matter where in the world I traveled.

I paid a hundred yen to a homeless man for the trash bag he carried as he searched for food and sake bottles in the trash as dawn broke in a back alley in Ginza, Tokyo.

I picked up trash can liners in the streets of Denmark, and thousands of miles away on another continent, in Patagonia, under the curious looks of people on the street. My bags consistently outperformed all the bags I found everywhere.

I believe the quality of my bags resulted from years of experience of being a student of resin quality, the processing know-how I learned and practiced during my years with Extrudo and Norchem, and my unyielding commitment to quality.

As the word spread about the superior quality of my bags, sales slowly picked up, then accelerated. My business began to grow.

Mary Underwood, the private-label purchasing manager of Safeway grocery stores, was starting up a new generic bag, Spring Field label program. She awarded me the contract. Bruce Daniel of United Grocers in Oakland, a large distributor, did the same.

Trans Western Polymers grew from $2 million in sales its first year in 1984 to $25 million by 1987. To meet what became a continuous demand, I moved to a larger facility, a new 120,000-square-foot building in Livermore, California.

God's blessing landed upon me once again.

I heard that Price Club, a new retailer that pioneered a new marketing concept for selling products in bulk, had opened a new regional buying office in Hayward. Its manager, Tom Martin, advised me to reach out to a house broker who managed procurement in San Diego named Ken Chamberlin.

I drove down to meet with Ken at his office near Price Club's headquarters just a few miles north of the San Diego airport. Ken, I found out, represented Presto, a competitor and a national supplier that monopolized the trash bag industry.

I found Ken to be personable from our first handshake.

Ken told me he was impressed with my products and would find a way to represent Trans Western Polymers someday. He then told me he was good friends with Jim Sinegal, one of the original Price club founders who had moved on and founded a new company called Costco in Kirkland, Washington in 1983.

Ken went with Jim. Soon after, Ken introduced me to Curt Newberry, vice president of merchandise, and they both toured my factory and inspected every part of my operation.

After in-depth testing in the lab and focus groups, Costco awarded its trash bag business to Trans Western Polymers.

It was a significant event that augured well for the future. Both of us, Costco and Trans Western, were about to grow exponentially.

CHAPTER TWENTY-FIVE

Costco

Costco was expanding rapidly across the country, in California, the Northwest, Southwest, Southeast, Midwest, Canada, and Mexico. It had plans to expand to the East by the early 1990s.

I wanted to learn as much as I could about Costco, its mission, code of ethics, merchandising strategies, and management principles. The founder and CEO, Jim Sinegal, was a great man with the highest integrity who valued his employees and customers. He had delivered the best value in goods to every Costco member.

I thought he was a great patriot, both as a citizen and businessman. He left nothing to chance and never isolated himself in an executive suite, delegating chores to others. It was no surprise Costco had grown so rapidly and had become the industry leader in such a short time.

Jim and his team attended every opening of a new Costco store. I knew because I participated in each one as well and always saw him there.

With Costco's explosive growth, there were plenty of new openings. We'd often meet at the front of the entrance, and Jim would say, "Good to see you again, Joon." On the morning of opening day at Fresno, California in 1985, I kidded Jim.

"Hey, Jim, I did not have breakfast at the hotel, so I came here to eat my meal from demo tables."

I'd work a Costco opening from 10:00 a.m. until the 8:30 p.m. closing time, doing demonstrations of my trash bag, the Commercial Strength brand. I'd call out to passing Costco members. "Hello, Ma'am (or Sir), have you tried the strongest and the most durable trash bag?" Then I'd stretch the bag to demonstrate its toughness.

Once, a young girl challenged me to show the bag would hold her. She stepped inside, and her father and I lifted her. The bag held her. She began her own sales pitch to passersby. "Look, everyone. This bag holds me up. I bet it can hold anything."

I must have met thousands of everyday people during each Costco demo week. After just a few words with each shopper, I was impressed, once again, that Americans are discriminating and thrifty shoppers who appreciate the value of products they purchase.

Soon after, Commercial Strength brand changed to private label "Kirkland Signature". The passion of Jim and his Costco employees demanded their label products deliver highest quality to their members on a consistent basis.

That was what my product offered.

CHAPTER TWENTY-SIX

The Poconos

With the Costco partnership blooming and Trans Western Polymers' portfolio growing, I quickly realized I had to expand my manufacturing capability in the eastern United States. I knew there was no trash bag maker capable of supplying Costco quality products within one thousand miles of the central-eastern region, where Costco was about to expand in the early 1990s.

I had been drawn to the Poconos in northeastern Pennsylvania since my first drive through the forested land to attend the national sales meeting in 1968.

I turned to Paul Nester, my sales broker in the East—and my good friend, who was known as the "Godfather" and spiritual mayor of Tamaqua, a small town near Allentown, Pennsylvania—to suggest a location for me.

Paul, enthusiastically, said that Tamaqua would make a perfect site for Trans Western Polymers, and he invited the directors of the Schuylkill County Economic Development Agency to pitch to me. They showed me a forty-acre parcel packed with tall pine trees. The minute I stepped on the beautiful lot, I once again thought of my hometown.

There was no indication at the time that Costco would award its eastern-region business to Trans Western Polymers. Nevertheless, I took the chance of a lifetime and decided to build a factory. I believed in my ability to succeed and in the audaciousness of my plans. As always, Kyuhee fully supported my decision, risking everything we had and our dream once again. That was the depth of our love for each other.

The construction of my factory in Tamaqua was completed in late 1995. In early 1996, Costco awarded me its eastern and midwestern business. The East Coast Costco regional manager spoke at the corporate manager's meeting, "If a man bet on the growth of Costco and built a new manufacturing facility to provide better service with all he had, he deserves our business."

The risk, when taken with God's blessing, proved worth it.

Tamaqua was an old coal-mining town with a high unemployment rate of more than 28 percent when the rest of the country was hovering near 9 percent. Its ethnic makeup was primarily German and Italian immigrants, many of whom had been through hard and trying times. Many had also retired from the work force since there was little work available.

I began on-the-job training with a handful of orders and only six workers. At the end of the first training day, we celebrated our first Christmas together at The Mother's, a local restaurant run by a lovely old lady named Mary.

Trans Western Polymers began manufacturing Costco orders in January 1996. It was difficult at the beginning. New employees were coming to work drunk, fighting in the parking lot, taking illegal drugs during breaks, stealing, reporting late for work, and worst of all, not showing up for shifts. They needed hope, and I realized the town and its residents had been down a long time.

I knew I had to be patient and understanding. So, I asked the county Economic Development Agency and the local Pennsylvania Labor Department for their support. Groups from both agencies spent weeks training the employees and educating them of their responsibilities and rights, legal considerations, family concerns, and how to resolve conflicts with their fellow workers and the supervisors.

I would visit the Tamaqua plant every other week and stay five days to train technicians, resolve every plant concern, take time to speak individually with each employee, conduct department manager meetings, continue work on expansion planning, and made time to visit Costco locations. Finally, after nearly six months, we resolved the human resource issues.

I had given these wonderful, hardworking people some light after so much darkness. It was incredibly gratifying. They would repay me with loyalty and gratitude.

The trips back East were trying, but I was motivated. I would leave home and my loving family in California at six o'clock in the morning, fly for six hours, then pick up a rental car and drive another three hours, and after a quick bite, arrive at a Fairfield Inn at around 10:00 p.m.

As soon as I showered and slid into bed, I would suffer painful leg cramps that lasted more than thirty minutes every night. I used a local Amish remedy to relieve the cramps. It took about fifteen minutes, but it never failed to work. With me sitting on the edge of my motel bed holding my throbbing legs in pain I would often ask myself, "These legs of mine took me from a little town in North Korea to a Fairfield Inn in Tamaqua, Pennsylvania. Why cramp now?"

The following day, after a few hours of sleep bolstered by bitter in-room coffee, I would arrive at the factory at 7:00 a.m. to greet some fifty night-shift workers at the exit door, where the timecard machine hung on the wall. I would happily and genuinely greet each worker with, "Thank you for doing a great job."

The workers, who naturally looked tired coming off their shift, would greet me with soft smiles. "How are you doing, Mr. Bai?" "Good to see you, Mr. Bai."

Those greetings made the long trip and my cramping legs worthwhile. I felt rejuvenated as I stood by the exit door and watched them drive away.

I'd return to my office, grab a cup of coffee, close my eyes, and think of Kyuhee and the kids for a few stolen moments from my hectic schedule.

Kyuhee always expressed her concerns about my travel, particularly driving the narrow and outdated Pennsylvania Turnpike at night, when truck traffic seemed to multiply.

We had taken many such drives together, so she knew driving on that highway on winter nights was very difficult. We had to follow large trucks, keep our eyes on the signs and road conditions, and stay alert throughout the drive.

Each time when I left home, she would pray that God would keep me safe.

I *promised* her that I would do my best to manage the new company, treat my workers honorably, and supply the finest quality products to my customers.

I felt Kyuhee's presence in my heart and heard her prayers.

CHAPTER TWENTY-SEVEN

Success at Last

My success in Tamaqua did not happen overnight, nor did it arrive by chance.

I would spend twenty years in northeastern Pennsylvania applying the principles that had served me well in business since the days I was a cigarette boy in Busan. I worked hard, was fair to my workers, provided better products to customers than my competitors, and was honest.

I simply followed my mother's teachings and Kyuhee's prayers. The success did not come easily, but it would arrive. Kyuhee stood by me, unwavering in her support and love, for those twenty years while I established my company and burnished its stellar reputation.

Tamaqua was strategically located to service Costco's new eastern territory, but so were other towns. I was determined to build a respectable company and help make Tamaqua a better place. I chose Tamaqua for my East Coast factory because its landscape was very much like where I had grown up, and at later year, I realized I made a right choice for all the beautiful people I met in Schuylkill County, Pennsylvania.

During those years, Kyuhee and I kept our family in California happy, healthy, and loving. Once again, it was with God's blessings.

I had hung a mission statement on the wall in front of my office for all to see. It read: "Keep our factory a safe place to produce quality products efficiently, compete fairly, and deliver reliable service to our customers with passion, we will then succeed."

At Trans Western, we hired previously unemployed workers, trained them, and watched as they became dependable and confident. Then we would reward them fairly, and by doing so, contribute to the community.

Of course, there were early years when expenses were higher than income, but I would give every worker a holiday bonus that matched ones from a previous profitable year. I will never forget their happy faces when they received bonus checks.

My relationship with my workers was exceptional. They were genuinely happy to see me, and I always had time to talk with them and listen to them, no matter how busy I was. When I made the three-hour drive from the Newark airport to Tamaqua, driving west on the Pennsylvania Turnpike after a long cross-country flight, the reception on the rental-car radio was terrible.

Hearing this, John, a night-shift packer, gave me a CD he had recorded of his favorite country-western music so that I could enjoy the ride back to the Newark airport. Genuine gestures like this made me feel good, realize the merits of my hard work, and gave me the joy of being the founder of such a vibrant enterprise.

Many of my people brought their family photos to share with me, and I was thrilled to see a wedding photo of a young couple, Barbara and Phil, who met during the start-up's early days, got married, and had a child.

Workers knew I wanted the workplace clean and safe, so they cleaned the entire facility until it sparkled before I arrived. The company grew reliably, and all my people and their families were happy to be a part of it.

The word spread far and wide.

Pennsylvania State Senator David Argall wrote to Costco Founder Jim Sinegal. "One day, a man with a strange name came to our town in Schuylkill County and turned it into a great place to work during the most economically challenging time."

We held our holiday party every year at Antonino's around Christmas. Neighboring companies were envious because we were the only ones in town celebrating.

The holiday parties were magnificent. All the women workers, who wore blue jeans on the factory floor, arrived in full-length dresses; some wore fancy high-top hats as they danced to the live band, Fosse's Steam Heat. Kyuhee and I walked over to each round table, shook hands, hugged, and shared holiday greetings.

Pennsylvania State Representative Jerry Knowles spoke during one party.

"The entire community in Schuylkill County greatly appreciates Mr. Bai's total contribution and his love for our people." He turned around and, looking at me, said, "Thank you, Mr. Bai." As he walked back to his chair, he touched my shoulder with an appreciative gesture. I accepted these accolades with gratitude. Kyuhee was sitting next to me, holding my hand. "Joon, I am so proud of you," she told me.

One of my most stringent principles was my unfaltering belief in offering consistency in quality in my products. I believed that was essential to my success.

Some competitors violated federal regulations that required all products to comply with the size and weight statement on their packages. I maintained rigorous standards. My major customers had focus groups that conducted weight and measure tests in their labs and households and found my bags always exceeded specifications.

As a result of the high regard in which I was held, a direct result of my reputation for integrity and quality, I was called to testify at a Securities and Exchange Commission hearing on a proposed merger between two giant chemical companies, Dow Chemical and Union Carbide.

Was there a conflict of interest in such a merger on the issue of manufacturing and marketing high-performance polyethylene resin, raw materials for plastic products? I was asked.

I was purchasing octene polyethylene resin from Dow and super hexene polyethylene resin from Union Carbide. We were using both high-performance resins for manufacturing Costco's Kirkland Signature private-label trash bags.

Our quality-assurance testing convinced me that the bags made by both resins performed equally well, producing identical bags in terms of mechanical properties of impact, tear, puncture, and surface friction. Accordingly, I reported at the hearing, that a merger between the two mega-chemical manufacturers would not violate antitrust laws.

On February 6, 2001, the Federal Trade Commission reported that Dow settled the antitrust issue relating to its proposed merger with Union Carbide. As a result, Dow Chemical purchased Union Carbide for $9.3 billion. Since then, the merger has given Dow an impetus to expand their market and, later, become the world's largest chemical company.

I learned from that incident that when three parties, the raw material producer (Dow), the fabricator (Trans Western Polymers), and the retailer (Costco), work together and find a common objective of delivering quality and valued products to the public, it is a striking example of the American economy at its best.

I also learned that, in America, you do not have to be dishonest to be profitable, you do not have to be greedy to succeed, and you do not have to bring down your competitors to be ahead of the pack.

With additional sales growth at Costco and securing new accounts like BJ's, by 2011, Trans Western Polymers became a company with over four hundred employees and $175 million in annual sales.

CHAPTER TWENTY-EIGHT

The Joy of Travel

Mark Twain once wrote that "Travel is fatal to prejudice, bigotry, and narrow-mindedness."

Kyuhee and I were born travelers. We both had worked so hard and so singularly toward success. We had both made tremendous sacrifices. Each of us had left the security of everything we loved to come to America, a country we barely knew, to take a big chance on finding the opportunities we had heard about but could only imagine.

It had taken great courage to chase our dreams, but we were undeterred and in love, knowing we had the strength of two. Bolstered by our faith in God and our courage to venture into the unknown, we had done so without hesitation while we learned about America.

My many travels had become a singular pursuit as I hopped across the country in my early years as I rose through the corporate ranks. Kyuhee, pursuing her nursing career, church activities, and caring for our sons, could not travel as much as she wished.

My travels were far from relaxing, especially when I was routinely flying to Pennsylvania as my company grew, established itself, and began operating smoothly. Those extended periods apart had been difficult for us because it was hard for each of us to separate for even a day. Once that difficult void began to close as my company grew, we decided to become travelers again.

During long flights to the Pennsylvania factory, I took up the happy chore of poring over travel magazines, studying the places Kyuhee would like to go. I picked historical and cultural places of interest. It was an easy and fun assignment because I knew Kyuhee enjoyed meeting people, seeing different landscapes, and learning about other cultures anywhere in the world.

We wanted to see the world and embark on a new set of adventures together. We chose countries where we could experience the unknown and be two inquisitive souls. It was time to enjoy the fruits of our labor, and we could not think of a better way than traveling.

My memories of the trips Kyuhee and I took together are golden and unfading, like clear and vibrant snapshots from a photo album I can open instantly at any time.

We were perfect traveling companions for each other, curious, intrepid, and undeterred by the usual complications of life on the road. We both were interested in learning as much as we could about the people and the cultures of the places we saw. And more than anything, we were with each other.

Nothing could be better.

CHAPTER TWENTY-NINE

Adventures around the World

Our first trip was to Austria and Switzerland in 1986.

We followed that in 1989 with a trip to Ireland.

Ireland's economy at the time was struggling, and unemployment was high, but we found the people open and friendly. After picking up our rental car at Shannon airport on a cloudy and drizzly day, my first challenge was to remember to drive on the left side of the road, especially when navigating the many traffic circles, or roundabouts as the Irish call them, on Ireland's narrow backroads. Once I became used to that, the slower pace of our trip through this beautiful country was just what we needed.

On our first night at Dromoland Castle in County Clare, we dressed formally for dinner, me in a suit and tie, Kyuhee in a lovely dress. There, we listened to the music of a woman in an Irish dress playing the harp. When the waitress leaned over my shoulder to place a glass of Irish whiskey in front of me, I saw two mountainous breasts in front of my eyes. I watched as Kyuhee tried her darndest not to laugh.

We saw much of Ireland and ate up its magical atmosphere. We drove to Killarney National Park, kissed the Blarney Stone, and had lunch at a little seaside restaurant, Aherne's, near Cork. The traditional Irish breakfasts and their copious amounts of thick bacon, eggs, and potatoes astounded us.

Kyuhee urged me to stop for teenage hitchhikers, mostly girls walking and holding hands. We enjoyed the friendly chats. Most of the girls told us that they wanted to immigrate to America. Kyuhee and the girls sang "Oh, Danny Boy," and as I drove, a wonderful chorus filled the car and spilled into the Irish countryside.

$\backsim$

I regularly attended the K-Show, the most extensive international trade show for the plastics industry, held every third year in Dusseldorf, Germany. I felt it was essential to keep up with new developments in industry technology. It is a seven-day show, but I usually stayed for three. Then Kyuhee and I would take advantage of the central location and visit other European countries.

Kyuhee often told me that she was intrigued by Spain's music, romance, and the passion of its people.

After she arrived in Chicago, she took up the classical guitar, performed at church, and gave concerts at local colleges.

We visited Spain after the 1991 K-Show in Dusseldorf. First, we toured the Museo Nacional del Prado in Madrid, filled with world-famous paintings. We stayed at the Paradores hotels in Segovia, Toledo, Cordova, Carmona (Seville), and Alhambra (Granada). In Cordova, we visited a mosque-cathedral, and in Seville, we took an outdoor stroll in the Plaza de Espana. Later that evening, we went to a small concert hall and saw a young guitarist playing the Concierto de Aranjuez. In Granada, we made a breathtaking tour of the Alhambra, "the red" palace, and fortress of the Moorish monarchs.

Even the smallest of events presented us with bright moments. In the narrow streets of Carmona, surrounded by high, stone walls, we had no landmark to direct us to our hotel. We saw a middle-aged woman walking with an infant on her back and holding a young girl's hand.

We gestured to the woman that we were lost. The woman gestured back to us to follow her. I held the girl's hand, and Kyuhee held the woman's hand and we walked together to our hotel some distance away. The woman and child then turned and made the long walk back to where we started. It took a while for us to say farewell, embracing each other again and again. The girl kept repeating, "Adios, Adios."

We took a side trip to Portugal, drove the coastal road through many small towns of Fatima, Battalion, and Obidos, and stopped by the food stand for Praca, Portuguese sausages.

Later in the evening, we dined at a well-known café in Lisbon and listened to Fado, a Portuguese music genre renowned for its expressive and profoundly melancholic character. We did not understand a word but watching the singer's facial and bodily expressions, we could feel the deep emotions of the song, much like Korean "Arirang."

⸎

Kyuhee suggested we visit South America for our next vacation. We chose to head off the beaten path to tour Chile's stunning Lake District, a region of snowcapped mountains and crystal-clear lakes, then into Argentina, and finally to Brazil.

From Santiago, Chile, we arrived in Puerto Montt after a long day of travel. We went straight to a seafood market to stay awake from jet lag, where I noticed a friendly fisherman shucking all kinds of shellfish, oysters, and sea urchins.

Sea urchins were my favorite, and Kyuhee smiled as she watched me bolt them down. The fisherman smiled as well and gestured at me as if he had never seen anyone devour sea urchins in that fashion. People at the market were lovely, and they refused to take my money, as much as I tried to pay.

We sailed across the startlingly green Lake Todos los Santos, hiked through the jungle, said adios to the Chilean hills, turned around, and said bienvenido as we stepped on the snow-covered Argentinean soil.

After a short bus ride, we arrived at the Hotel Llao Llao, which sat by a beautiful green lake, and took a quick boat ride to the magnificent falls in Bariloche, Argentina. From there, a short flight took us to the Iguazu Falls.

There, we took a powerboat ride from the Argentinean side under the roaring and immense Iguazu, perhaps the most beautiful waterfall in the world. The next day we walked the rim of the falls from Brazilian side. It was awe-inspiring, unlike anything we had ever seen. That moment was precisely the reason Kyuhee and I loved to travel together, to share those special moments only we would talk about forever.

In the boat under the falls, Kyuhee, with moisture dripping from her full raincoat, turned to me and said, "Human beings can't create such magnificent wonder."

That night in the hotel's main lounge, I sat drinking Torrontes, a local white wine, as I watched Kyuhee dance tango to "Por Una Cabeza" with a handsome young professional Argentinian dancer. I wished I could dance like Argentinians.

We flew from Buenos Aires, Argentina, to Rio de Janeiro, Brazil. On that afternoon, I sat in the busy lobby of the Copacabana Hotel in Rio de Janeiro, waiting for Kyuhee to come down from our room.

It seemed, quite inadvertently, that we had timed our visit to coincide with that of President Bill Clinton's. The two sets of elevator doors opened simultaneously in a moment that I could not have choreographed more perfectly if I had tried. From one emerged Kyuhee; from the second, President Clinton.

As soon as she saw that familiar face, she recognized it was Clinton. She turned to me as if to say, "Am I seeing who I think I'm seeing?" She turned to Clinton.

"Hi, Mr. President, how are you doing? What are you doing in Rio?" she called out.

With his typical crafty smile, President Clinton responded kindly, "I am doing fine. I am here for the conference."

Then, the president, reporters, and secret service walked toward the famed Copacabana beach, where tall, chocolate-skinned beautiful girls danced and played volleyball under the sun.

We thought Rio de Janeiro was one of the most beautiful cities in the world.

～

The never-ending conflicts of the Middle East had intrigued me for years.

I decided I wanted to see for myself the source of what I had been reading about Christians and Muslims. Kyuhee was with me all the way. We were an intrepid pair.

In 1994, we headed to the United Arab Emirates, Oman, Syria, Jordan, and Lebanon. We traveled through the desert and drank dark coffee at Bagdad Café 66 on the Syrian-Jordan border. We climbed the steps of Bel-Temple at Palmyra, breathed desert air at the top of Krak des Chevaliers castle, and imagined the Saladin's warriors circling the fort.

At Petra, a historic archaeological site in Jordan and one of the Seven Wonders of the World, we chose to walk the three kilometers to the temple rather than ride camels, so we could see and appreciate every corner of the limestone valley in silence and feel the light breeze.

We had a Zarb, a Bedouin traditional lunch of assorted baked lamb, goat, chicken, and vegetables, and on our way back, we stopped by the side of the road where a boy was selling small stones, more like pebbles.

I was chatting with Ramsey, a guide, who was brushing down a camel. When I looked around, I found Kyuhee was buying all the boy's stones and placing them in her bag.

When we reached the camel carriage to depart, Kyuhee gave the bag of stones to the driver to return to the boy so he could sell them again.

～

Inspired by our favorite TV programs, *National Geographic*, *Nature*, and *Animal Kingdom*, we traveled to Zambia, Zimbabwe, Botswana, and South Africa in 1995.

I had said to Kyuhee earlier, "Before our steps slow down and traveling the wilderness becomes more difficult, how about we go see the animals in the endless plain, Serengeti?"

We stood at the edge of the awesome Victoria Falls wearing raincoats to keep us from being soaked from the mists shooting skyward, and we drank champagne on Livingstone Island at the rim of the falls, watching the sunset.

In South Africa, we visited Robben Island, a thirty-minute boat ride from Cape Town, to tour the maximum-security prison cell where Nelson Mandela was imprisoned for eighteen of his twenty-seven years of incarceration. The tour guide told us that all six of the volunteer guides, now in their eighties, had gone to university with Mandela and fought to end apartheid, South Africa's rigid racial separation policy that had deprived its majority Black population of so much for years.

We saw our guide cry at one spot describing how he was tortured during his prison days. "Do you cry every time?" I asked. The guide said he conducts the tour once a day, six days a week, and cries every time. I saw Kyuhee was deeply saddened to hear the price these people had to pay for their freedom. We, too, had tears in our eyes.

∽

A TV documentary on Chilean Patagonia impressed us so much we chose to go there for our 1996 trip, to see firsthand its stunning landscape and nature.

After a long flight, we arrived at the port town of Punta Arenas near the southern tip of Patagonia. From there, we took a long and bumpy bus ride to Torres del Paine National Park, home to guanacos, pumas, and llama-like animals. It was known for its high mountains, green lakes, glaciers, pampas, and grasslands.

Keeping adventurous in such a pristine setting, Kyuhee took the opportunity to hike trails under the imposing mountains.

We took a sailing excursion through the waters of Beagle Channel, where we were amazed by the Avenue of the Glaciers. We disembarked in a smaller inflatable Zodiac and visited Cape Horn, the lowest point in the South American continent. On the way, we said hello to tiny penguins, which looked the same as the ones we said goodbye to at the beautiful Boulders Beach in South Africa, near Cape Point years before.

We thanked God for allowing us to travel and explore this wonderful earth of ours.

☙

In Sicily, in 1997, driving from Syracuse to Agrigento, we stopped at the small town of Piazza Armerina to have a glass of wine. The December day was sunny and warm. We sat at a small table next to a couple of local elders. Unexpectedly, a wedding parade passed by.

The scene was right out of *The Godfather*, when Michael Corleone married a Sicilian girl, Apollonia. The groom wore a dark suit with a white boutonniere, and the bride, holding a bouquet, wore a beautiful white wedding dress. Dozens of family members and friends were following them, keeping pace with the sound of a trumpet.

I took a sip and turned to look at Kyuhee and took her hands in mine.

"Let us marry again."

"Yes," she said, nodding her head, just as she did when I proposed for the first time.

The Sicilian seniors smiled at us as if to say, "Congratulations."

We were once again at The Top of the Rock in Chicago, overlooking Lake Michigan. It was as if time had stood still.

☙

We married a second time on our twenty-fifth wedding anniversary in September 1989, at the grand ballroom of the Marriott Hotel, in San Ramon, California. James and Steve roasted us in front of over two hundred joyful relatives and friends. Everybody applauded as they called out, "Kiss, kiss."

Recalling her borrowed wedding dress, Kyuhee looked at me while we danced. "Joon, I am so happy. I am wearing all new. I do want you to know that I was so happy at our first wedding," she said.

I whispered in her ear, "How about we marry again at our fiftieth anniversary at the Fern Grotto in Kauai?"

"Yes," Kyuhee replied, nodding her head and flashing a happy smile.

In 1999, we traveled to Egypt to see the opera *Aida* in Gaza and to experience Cairo, a Nile cruise, and to tour Luxor, Aswan Dam, and Abu Simbel.

In the shadow of the pyramids in the cool evening air, *Aida*, Giuseppe Verdi's masterwork, was magnificent. Performed by the Italian Opera with a thousand Egyptian special military units as extras, it was nothing short of perfect.

Aida recounts the wrenching forbidden love of Radamès, a young Egyptian warrior, and Aida, an Ethiopian princess who is captured and detained in Egypt as a slave. It is a story of heartbreak and betrayal, set during a war between Egypt and Ethiopia. It is a timeless story of forbidden romance.

Early the next morning Kyuhee and I mounted two very large camels, Kyuhee on a female named Rosy.

Riding a camel itself is an experience, even before you begin to move. Camels stand from the sitting position using their front legs. As they rise, the riders are first thrown backward with a jolt, then forward with equal force as the camel's back legs engage. It is not unlike sitting in a slingshot, and it is important to have a firm grip on the saddle to avoid being thrown off. If accomplished successfully, the ride is as smooth as silk.

Once we were up and moving, our ride became sublime, unforgettable. In moments, we were a caravan of two without a guide, riding together gracefully to the pyramids. As we neared the pyramids, Kyuhee reached over, grabbed my hand, placed it in hers, and raised our joined arms together.

"Joon, you are my eternal love. I wish time would stop and let this moment last forever," she said loudly for the world to hear.

I turned to her. "Kyuhee, our love will be eternal," I *promised* her.

CHAPTER THIRTY

Sons

Years later, we would take another family vacation, this time at the behest of Kyuhee, who wanted the entire family to travel together. James and Steve were in college, at NYU and Columbia in New York City. We found a time when they could join us and went to Cancun, a Caribbean beach resort on Mexico's Yucatan Peninsula.

On our second day, James, Steve, and I took an hour scuba diving lesson at the hotel pool, then hopped aboard a boat for a sea dive. After a thirty-minute boat ride to the open sea, all of us jumped in and dropped thirty-five feet, equalizing the pressure on the way down.

Sitting on the sandy ocean floor, my mask began to leak. I swam to the surface and climbed on the boat to find James sitting on the deck in a chair. He said he was uncomfortable in the dark sea.

On the other hand, Steve took to the water and stayed under for a long time, swimming like Johnny Weissmuller and shooting videos. That afternoon off Cancun was the beginning of a lifelong pursuit for Steve, who has become an avid diver, traveling the world to dive.

James is an artist, creative and curious. He showed an interest when Kyuhee enrolled him in in violin school when he was quite young. He is talented in art, music, and writing.

James put together a small rock band in high school and played at the local pizza places, singing and playing guitar. He made a good Elvis.

James graduated from San Diego State University with a major in economics and worked for a short time at an accounting firm. But his heart was not in it.

The arts were calling to him. One day he asked me if he could go to Columbia University in New York City to study film direction. Given my fascination with the movies that had begun in Busan as a young man, and my desire to learn film myself, I quickly gave James my blessing, as I did to Stephen. I wanted them to follow their passions.

James graduated with a master's degree in direction. He wrote an ingenious and creative script for a science-fiction love story, *Puzzlehead*, then produced and directed a full-length movie. *Puzzlehead* won the Best Feature Film award in the Science Fiction Film Festival at Trieste, Italy in 2005 and Jury Award at Austin Fantastic Festival. James entered it in several film competitions, including New York's elite Tribeca Film Festival, where he showed it to an audience of three hundred.

When the lights went on after the showing, he was greeted with enthusiastic applause.

During the Q and A, James talked about overcoming the many challenges of making a film as an Asian-American. He then thanked me for my support. I thought James was the proudest young man in Manhattan that night.

His father was very proud as well. I felt I was the one who was recognized that night. The film was sold to a distributor and ran on Netflix for many years.

James is married to Annie, a graduate of NYU law school, with whom he has three good-looking teenage boys, Luke, Jonah, and Aaron, (seventeen, fifteen, and thirteen) all passionate ice hockey players.

James continues to write screenplays and produce documentary films and pursue his passion for music, singing, playing guitar, and directing a small band at local gathering places.

Stephen is a very private and self-motivated young man. He first attended the University of Southern California. During his sophomore year, he was pulled by the arts and transferred to New York University's Tisch School of Art, a prestigious and selective film school, to study direction.

I can only imagine both boys' desire to become film directors came from my DNA and passion for film, which I consider a special gift.

Steve graduated from NYU and lived in an apartment two blocks from the World Trade Center on September 11, 2001. He shot the horrifying scenes with his video: the fires, pieces of building hitting the pavement, clouds of dust, and the wailing of fire trucks and ambulances. The most heartbreaking sounds were the cries of people falling from the World Trade Center.

He survived the traumatic attacks but could never return to his apartment. He moved to California and later married Jennifer, who he met at a Hapkido martial arts studio during his years in New York.

Steve worked for me for over twelve years as president of Trans Western Polymers and now manages his own investment business. Stephen has one son, Ian, seventeen years old; he is a champion debater, a top swimmer, and team and single sculls rower.

In 2000, Steve and I went to Kenya and Tanzania for what was a magical safari. We saw lions killing buffalo and a cheetah mother tending to her babies. We looked down from a hot-air balloon carrying us over the stunning Serengeti. The most beautiful bird in the world, the Queen Peacock, greeted us at the Kenya Safari Club, once owned by William Holden. We shook hands with the head of the Masai Mara and tribal members who came out to greet us, singing and dancing. We drank local wine under Mount Kilimanjaro in the cool afternoon, just as Hemingway did.

We had a frightening and memorable moment when the most enormous elephant I had ever seen charged the Jeep we were riding in. She roared and rushed toward us, leaving her baby behind, and stopped only a few feet away, screeching and raising her two front feet high. It was paralyzing.

After whipping her trunk and shaking her head violently, she walked away. When I saw our guide, Max, crouching and looking scared, I knew such a vicious attack by an elephant was rare. Max explained to us that she was protecting her baby.

Steven later told me it was the scariest experience in his life.

CHAPTER THIRTY-ONE

A Higher Calling

The news was devastating, and to me, painfully personal.

Driving home on Highway 580 West to Danville, California one afternoon in early January 1997, I was caught in a deluge. The sudden cloudburst exploded so forcefully I could barely make out the cars just yards in front of me. The rain continued with such power that cars slowed, then stopped and waited for the rain to let up.

As I sat distractedly watching my car's wipers sprint back and forth across the windshield, I listened to a report on public radio station KQED out of San Francisco saying that one hundred thousand North Korean children had died of starvation in the past year.

The number was incomprehensible. A single child dying is painful, and so many dying because of circumstances beyond their control was beyond tragic.

Years of continuous droughts had resulted in North Korea's worst harvest in history. In addition, the economic collapse of Russia had resulted in North Korea losing supplies of crude oil, natural gas, and fertilizer for the first time since its independence.

North Korea had stood alone for decades, following its Juche ideology. The country had only minimal trade with China and a few other nations, and no economic partners other than Russia, which was struggling itself economically. It had no plans to combat natural disasters such as droughts. The poor harvest had left its people on the verge of calamity.

Kyuhee and I found the harsh news difficult to accept. Thoughts of so many ordinary people in such dire circumstances haunted me for days. I could not sleep, thinking deep into the night, unable to shake the thought that so many children in my hometown had died of hunger. I knew I had to do something, and Kyuhee agreed.

We decided that I should return to Haeryong to see the extent of the peril. I also wanted to learn if I would be allowed to help and what, precisely, the North Korean government would allow me to do.

A friend, Park Un Sick, who had visited his uncle in North Korea the previous year, told me the best way to obtain a visa to the country was to send gifts, preferably food, to the Overseas Compatriot Ministry in Pyongyang.

Soon after, I purchased one forty-foot container load of one thousand cartons of Toast'em Pop-Ups pastries from the Schulze & Burch Biscuit Company in Chicago, where Park worked as a purchasing manager. That translated to more than five hundred thousand individual baked pastries that could be eaten right out of the package.

At Park's suggestion, I called a church elder in Los Angeles who ran a freight forwarding business and asked him to arrange shipment to North Korea through Chinese channels. After a weeklong negotiation, the container left Chicago for Pyongyang by way of Hong Kong and Beijing.

The container arrived at the Ministry of Education in Pyongyang one week before April 15, the Day of the Sun, the birthday of their greatest leader, and its founding father, Kim Il Sung. It had become North Korea's most celebrated day.

I had no idea if the container would arrive before the celebration, nor did I know April 15 is the Day of Sun, but the timing was fortuitous.

The pastries were perfect snacks for the thousands of school children after the day-long parade that started and ended at Kim Il Sung Square on a warm April day. The Ministry expressed its deep appreciation, stating how thoughtful I was in sending the most appropriate gifts on a well-chosen day.

The North Korean government issued me one entry visa to the Democratic People's Republic of Korea. Family and friends immediately expressed concerns about my trip. "Joon, be careful traveling to an unpredictable and dangerous country," they warned me. My brother Carl was distraught and begged me not to go.

"God will be with me every step of the way, so please, do not worry," I responded to everyone.

In the summer of 1997, I flew to Seoul, transferred to a flight to Yanji, China, then President Zhao drove me to Tumen City, China; the final leg was to cross a bridge on foot to Haeryong. As experienced as I was with travel and its unpredictability, the trip was tense and filled with anxiety. I did not know what awaited me.

After two days, I arrived in my hometown for the first time since I had left fifty years before, in 1947.

CHAPTER THIRTY-TWO

Orphans

I would soon see vivid and wrenching confirmation of the news I had heard on KQED earlier that year.

Two guides from the Overseas Compatriot Ministry in Pyongyang met me at Nam Yang, the border city with China, and escorted me on a tour of the Haeryong area. I witnessed thousands of children in orphanages and saw stark evidence of food shortages and suffering farmers at local communes. Local government officials I met had a simple message.

"Mr. Bai, we know you were born in the city of Haeryong, the birthplace of our mother. You are our brother who happens to live in a foreign country. Please help us."

The "mother" they referred to was Kim Jung Sook, the wife of the great leader Kim Il Sung and the mother of Kim Jong Il. A small cottage where she was born is now a museum, and a ten-foot bronze statue of her stands in the city plaza.

Their welcoming comments made me feel as if I had never left my hometown. I stayed for four days at a hotel where leaders stayed when they visited the area.

In what were presumably pre-arranged settings, I toured two orphanages, one senior nursing home, and four communal farms. At each stop, I would be greeted by local guides who would speak about what I would see, then praise their great leaders, Kim Il Sung and Kim Jung Il.

In Chongjin, North Korea's second-largest city, a half day's drive from Haeryong, we met the director of the Ae Uk Won orphanage, who told me they were desperately short of food, medical supplies, and clean water. One or two children died every night from malnutrition and diarrhea, she said. She related a scene of unimaginable horror.

"Our young nurses stack up many dead babies behind a barn, cover them with hay, unable to bury them in the frozen ground, and leave them in the winter. Then, when spring brings warmer temperatures and melts the snow and ice, they bury tens of frozen dead bodies."

My plans to help quickly began to take shape.

On my way back home to California, I stopped in Yanji, China, and met with Zhao Guang Xun and Ahn Mi Hwa, two Korean-Chinese I had known for years, to discuss what goods to purchase and deliver to the orphanages.

We visited wholesale markets in Yanji and Tumen City, across the Tumen River from Haeryong, to procure children's clothing and shoes, then arranged freight forwarders to pack and ship them.

Ms. Ahn arranged to ship four forty-foot containerloads of powdered milk for infants, flour, corn, corn oil, cabbage, turnips, dried fruits, and other essential items to four orphanages. These included diapers, socks, shoes, winter clothes, soap, plastic bowls, insecticide powder, and other miscellaneous needs, of which there were many.

We could not send rice because China, at the time, was in the midst of a shortage, making it non-exportable. All the containers arrived at the orphanages, one in Haeryong, two in Chongjin, and one in Kilju.

We were off to a good start but faced an avalanche of paperwork and logistical burdens. For efficiency in managing what I hoped to be a continuing aid program, I felt I needed to go to Pyongyang and discuss my plans with the of Overseas Compatriot Ministry.

I knew from my years in sales that a face-to-face meeting would make it easier to get the government support I needed—permits for the shipments, visas for my entry, capable guides, and assistance to obtain crucial local government support.

My son James had become curious and very interested in my work in North Korea and asked several times if he could join me on my future trips. With his mother's blessing, I agreed. North Korea issued a visa for James without any delay. We had much work to do.

CHAPTER THIRTY-THREE

Getting to Work

Under my direction, my team in Yanji, China would deliver much-needed goods to four orphanages twice a year for four years, from 1997 to 2000.

I was continually looking for ways to make each delivery more efficient and effective. One of the orphanage directors, Ms. Lee, was a tall and thin woman in her early sixties who smiled softly, spoke gently, greeted me warmly, and told me about the orphanages she managed. I spoke with her and her staff about shipments they would receive, and how to verify quantities, the condition of the goods on arrival, and the things they would need urgently in the next shipment.

Ms. Lee led me to a dozen orphans' rooms, one by one. A nurse handed me an effusive baby girl who seemed transfixed by the appearance of this friendly stranger.

The baby kept looking at me. I said to her, "Would you like to go to America with Grandpa?" The baby looked at me curiously as if she understood me. That made the nurses laugh. In my heart, I wished I could bring her and all those beautiful orphans back home to America.

I asked one of the nurses to take photos of me with all the kids in each room. The children, having never seen a camera, didn't seem to know what was going on. They stared, unsmiling, even after I acted as a clown to try to make them laugh. They had not smiled for a long time. I thought to myself, they had simply forgotten how.

∽

In my meetings with Ms. Lee and her staff, I encouraged them to express, openly, their challenges and the needs of their children. Toward the end of each meeting, Ms. Lee, smiling, would read a list of goods they had received in a loud voice. "We received all the goods that we asked for, thank you. We will never forget your love for our children," she told me.

On one visit, Ms. Lee asked me if I could send her a gas-powered chain saw. I thought it was non-essential item and I asked her why she would need a power saw. She called a nurse into the room and asked her to open her palms. The nurse, wearing a white uniform with what looked like a high chef's toque, walked over to me and opened her palms.

I was shocked at her scarred and bloody hands. They were the result of trying to cut wood from a frozen tree with a hammer, bare-handed, to provide shards of wood to heat the rooms. Those small bits of wood were the only source of heat for the infants.

The nurse said that farmers had already cut down the smaller trees nearby and nurses were forced to climb a great distance high into the mountains to find anything to cull. There were only large trees remaining. The only source of heat for the infants was the small bits of wood a nurse could painfully chip off with a hammer.

I could not forget that nurse with her angelic face and her small, white, bloody scar-covered hands. I held her hands and prayed that the power of love from my hands would flow into hers and heal them quickly. The nurse looked just like my Kyuhee in her white uniform.

I told the director that the sacrifices of her young volunteer nurses under the most challenging situation had touched me. I asked the director if I could give any gifts to these young volunteers. The director said, "That is very thoughtful of you. If you wish, you could give them blankets."

"Why blankets?" I asked.

"In our tradition, the bride-to-be brings a gift to her wedding, usually blankets," she told me.

I sent two dozen blankets in the next container, the best gift I have ever given to anyone. The container also included four gas-powered chain saws.

∽

In April 1998, waiting in the Air Koryo departure lounge in the old Beijing airport, a man who must have heard us speaking, approached me and said, in Korean, "You must be going to Pyongyang with your son. Why are you taking him to such a dangerous place?"

I quickly looked for James who was away reading a book and was relieved to see he had not heard the rather ominous remark. James and I had spoken about the dangers of the trip before, and after the man's comment I asked him again.

"James, do you feel uncomfortable going to Pyongyang?"

He left little room for doubt. "Dad, I am going to our homeland with you, right?"

When we arrived in Pyongyang, I saw the director and guides in the Overseas Compatriot Ministry were delighted to have a second-generation Korean-American coming to his parents' birthplace.

At a dinner to celebrate our arrival, James went around the table and poured wine for the high-level officials, normally not a Korean tradition. No one minded, though, and officials seemed to appreciate the gesture. The director raised his glass and toasted the moment.

"We welcome Bai Sung Gook (James' Korean name), the first of the second-generation of Korean-Americans to visit the republic. We hope that many more of our sons and daughters living in faraway countries come to their parents' birth land."

During our stay in Pyongyang, James was given tours of several historical places, hiked Moran Mountain, and visited orphanages and visited local farming communities. He developed a good rapport with his guide, Mr. Lim.

I watched later at the airport departure gate as James gave Lim an English-Korean dictionary as a farewell gift. They hugged each other with tears in their eyes.

On the first leg of our flight back home, on our way to Beijing, James turned to me.

"Dad, thank you for taking me to our motherland."

I was grateful as well. We had established a trusting relationship with Pyongyang, and my effort to aid orphanages was moving ahead smoothly with no hitches.

CHAPTER THIRTY-FOUR

Challenging Journeys

My many trips to Haeryong called for every bit of stoicism and serenity Kyuhee and I had acquired over our many years and hundreds of thousands of miles of travel.

Our journeys to North Korea to help the orphans were quite unlike anything we had done before. Any rewards or recognition would make us feel uncomfortable. We did it simply because our hearts called for it.

In 1997, I was the only person carrying a US passport to cross the Tumen Byung Gang Bridge at Nam-Yang, which I called the Unification Bridge, two hundred meters long, to enter North Korea. After a farewell to my staff, I walked over the bridge to Nam Yang City, North Korea, alone, on foot, pulling a small traveling suitcase.

I crossed that bridge more than twenty times from 1997 to 2013.

The bridge had a thin, white painted line marking precisely equidistance between two countries, the border between China and North Korea. It was an eerie experience crossing. I could hear only the sound of the heavy wind and feel the cold air drifting south from Siberia.

At the end of the bridge on the North Korean side, I would pass a small security post the size of a telephone booth guarded by a soldier who appeared to be in his mid-teens. With a rifle hanging over his shoulder, he greeted me with an energetic salute.

We were not allowed to talk and only looked at each other as I passed. I would flash him a "happy-to-see-you-again" smile. He would respond with a thin, shy smile on his dark face to express the same sentiment. I imagine seeing me was the young border guard's only excitement for the day.

I never saw individual traders or any other pedestrians crossing that bridge. Each time I saw that boy soldier, I was struck by the contrasts. Me, an older man born in the nearby town who had lived fifty years in the United States, and him, a boy with an uncertain future guarding the border of two countries, who likely knew very little. I wanted to hug him.

Every two years of crossing the bridge, I would see another young soldier who looked just like the one he replaced and he would greet me the same as his predecessor.

∽

My trips to that part of North Korea required two visas, one each from China, and North Korea, a process that generally takes weeks. Unfortunately, there were no multiple-entry visas at the time.

Heading into that isolated part of the world, I carried a medical kit. There were no urgent care clinics, no emergency transportation such as ambulances or helicopters, and no cell phones. Cell phones were not permitted in the entire country. I had to deposit my phone at the entry customs and pick it up when I departed the country.

There were three ports of entry into North Korea, two by land and one by air. By land, there was Sinuiju City near the Lulu River in the northwestern tip of the country and Nam-Yang by the Tumen River in the northeastern-most corner of the country.

By air, there was a Pyongyang airport, and transport had to be on North Korea's national carrier, Air Koryo. So, from San Francisco, I would fly to Inchon, then to Yanji, where President Zhao Guang Xun drove me to the border immigration office in Tumen city to clear my departure on the Chinese side.

Every fall and spring, I visited the orphanages twice a year for nine years, from 1997 to 2005. From 2006 on I visited once a year until 2013. I wanted to see that the children were well cared for and that the goods I had sent provided for their urgent needs. I continued to provide aid until 2017 when the North Korean government would no longer allow it.

I instructed Ms. Ahn in Yanji to go to the Chinese-North Korean border-control offices on both sides to sign off on the permits, obtain receipts, and verify the deliveries in person every time forty-foot container trucks passed through.

Zhao Guan Xun, who later became the president of my new company, Trans Western Yanbian, in Tumen City, managed the funds I wired to him and coordinated the purchasing and shipping.

∽

My trips would follow a predictable sequence. After I crossed the bridge, I entered the customs office in North Korea. The people there knew who I was from my frequent visits. They always expressed their appreciation to me, shouting in unison, "We thank you for your unconditional donations for our people."

Then, the first officer would ask me, kindly, to empty my pockets. He then checked my wallet and other personal belongings, looked through every photo clip in my camera, glanced through the notes, and finally patted me down. They wanted to ensure I was not carrying a Bible or papers with Bible verses or other religious material.

Another officer would check the five thousand US dollars that I usually carried in one-hundred-dollar bills, then ask me if I had any more cash in two other currencies, Chinese Yen or Euros. North Korea accepted only these three currencies, no credit cards. He then would ask me how much money I planned to have on my return.

"I will spend it all in my hometown with pleasure," I would say.

"That is wonderful," the officer would shout.

North Korean agents I knew well from previous trips would greet me as I left the customs building. Agent Shin Sang Hwa from the Overseas Compatriot Ministry (OCM) in Pyongyang, responsible for guiding and overseeing my activities during my stay, welcomed me warmly.

Other agents included a man from the provincial government's same department, OCM, and a local government officer. Two other men, one I suspected to be an intelligence officer, and the other a driver, made up a contingent of five supervisors for me. When Zhao Guang Xun traveled with me, there would be another intelligence officer and a driver, all together eight of us in two cars.

To reach Haeryong, we drove in an old, beat-up Toyota for approximately three hours, a distance that would take less than an hour if the roads were well maintained. We drove over and around large potholes in dirt roads and over the temporary wooden bridges and under broken-down concrete bridges.

It was always a trying journey, but the opportunity to help the orphans made it selfishly happy travel.

CHAPTER THIRTY-FIVE

An Alien Landscape of Hope

Kyuhee would sometimes accompany me on my many trips. She was as invested as I was in brightening the future of those orphans.

The contrasts between our pleasant life in California and Haeryong were stark. North Korea was an alien landscape I learned early on my journeys that I needed to navigate carefully. My concern was not my safety but the well-being of the orphans I had grown to love. I would tread carefully to make sure I did not offend anyone and put my mission in jeopardy.

Driving through Haeryong, I saw many anti-American posters on billboards at the corners of intersections and on the sides of tall buildings. Most posters were histrionic, depicting American soldiers attacking North Korean civilians or Uncle Sam ripping the North Korean flag with a spear.

City life lacked modern touches. Women balanced large bundles of goods tied in cloth on their heads. Others carried their wares in pushcarts. Haeryong's main streets were paved with concrete, but side streets were hard-packed dirt.

We would always stay at Haeryong's only hotel, an uninspiring three-story building with a big reception hall. Kyuhee and I were often the only guests. Dinners were far from sumptuous, often a rice bowl, a small fried fish, kimchee, and vegetable soup.

I would stay in the hotel's grand suite, the same rooms where the Great Leaders stayed. In addition to a bedroom, the suite had a large living room and a bathroom, each dimly lit by a bare, low-wattage light bulb hanging unadorned from a wire that dropped from the ceiling. I could manage to see where I was going but could not read a book in what passed as a well-lit room at dusk.

The bed had a beautifully carved frame holding a thin mattress. After my long, bumpy rides, any bed would have been satisfactory for my weary body.

The toilet handle was rusted and broken. I would scoop water from the tub with a wooden bucket and pour it into the toilet reservoir to flush. Rooms always seemed cold, so I slept with my clothes on and used my jacket as an extra blanket.

One night I was awakened by a noise in the bathroom. I turned on the light and saw two giant rats running around the tub. I just went back to sleep; nothing would have bothered my tired soul that night.

Breakfast would usually consist of one piece of bread and a hard-boiled egg with instant coffee for me and hot jook, Korean rice soup, for my guides.

These were mere inconveniences compared with the tasks at hand and the reason I visited North Korea. They were inconsequential. Kyuhee and I were there to help, and there was a great need for it. The number of orphans was mind-boggling.

The orphans would arrive at their new homes by a grim and macabre selection process. First, because of the famine, government agents would regularly search the town for recently deceased adults. The statistics were shocking. On any given day, as many as twenty children, some infants, would be moved. Some would not survive.

Caretakers would not know how long the parents had been deceased. When they arrived to pick up the surviving babies, they would find them holding their dead parents, some sucking their deceased mother's breast, crying, and refusing to let go.

Caretakers would try to search for the children's names through town birth records, but when information was not available, the task of naming the new charge fell on the orphanage director.

Many of those babies did not understand what had happened to their parents. When they arrived at the orphanage, healthy babies cried all night, but a few silent ones barely opened their mouths as they approached their last breath.

CHAPTER THIRTY-SIX

Hope Grows

On one trip, we headed to Chongjin, the second-largest city in North Korea and the capital of northeastern Ham Kyung Book-Do Province, to visit two orphanages, Ae-Uk-Won, which cared for younger children up to age four, and Uk-Ah-Won, which cared for five- to eight-year-olds.

At Ae-Uk-Won, forty babies, newborns to two years old, were kept in ten large rooms about twice the size of an average American suburban living room. Each baby was covered in blankets as they lay on the Korean-style floor.

Because of an inappropriate diet and unpurified drinking water, the most common cause of death in the orphanages was diarrhea, because cities and towns did not have water purification plants nor any means to chlorinate.

And the babies could not digest the only food available, Kong Jook, a plain, mild soup made of wheat mixed with finely ground corn, filtered through a fine cloth. The babies were fed warm powdered milk only on rare occasions, a special day, such as the Great Leader's birthday.

Older children, three and four years old, were not immune to the diarrhea that assaulted their younger companions. They would sit on the floor in a circle, eating the remains of Kong Jook from large and unsanitary plastic bowls that were also used to wash dishes and diapers. They, too, would die of diarrhea.

I was the only male the orphans had seen since their fathers. Except for one elderly physician, everyone working in the orphanages was a woman, mostly young. As my visits became regular, these children would call out "Father, Father" when they saw me, some in strong and loud voices, others weakly.

Starting in the fall of 1997, my supply trucks would regularly bring food to these orphanages, and after a year, I was gratified to see pink cheeks and smiling faces. I also noticed the nurses, angels in white uniforms, looked happy and wore bright smiles as they devoted themselves to caring for those babies. The nurses were all young and pretty, so very much like a young nurse named Kyuhee, whom I had met so many years before in Chicago.

Those orphanage visits were nonetheless trying. It was wrenching to see so many young children, without parents, in such dire conditions. The day after a visit, I would wake before sunrise, then kneel by the bed and pray to God to bless me and give me the power of love and wisdom to help those poor souls.

Once, overcome, I wept with abandon, sobbing like an inconsolable child for nearly an hour. I prayed to God to show me the way. As I wept, I heard my mother saying, "Joon, love your neighbor," and Kyuhee's voice noted, "You are the son of God. It is your mission to help the poor."

God's words came to my mind, "Blessed are the pure in heart, for they will see God," "Blessed are the peacemakers, for they will be called sons of God."

My guide, Comrade Shin, knocked on the door and asked me if everything was okay.

∽

At Uk-Ah-Won, I saw about thirty children, ages five to eight, in a room. As with other visits, I saw one child was sitting on a toilet in the corner while others waited their turn, obviously due to running diarrhea.

I reached out to touch their hands and said, "Hello." They looked at me without expression and wondered who this man was, but they didn't seem afraid of me.

In addition to food, every year I also donated summer and winter clothes, socks, shoes, mattresses, blankets, soap, and other essential things kids that age would need. Other things I sent included hair clippers, rice cookers, and industrial washing machines.

As my visits continued, I witnessed an incredible chain reaction of events that gave me hope.

As those young children received the proper nutrition, they became healthy and began to engage in more outdoor activities. I sent soccer balls and goal posts, volleyballs and nets, and sports uniforms. As a result of all that exertion, they took more frequent baths, and their uniforms needed more frequent washing, so they were consuming more body and powdered soaps.

Playing soccer on hard dirt wears down shoes quickly. But those children were so accustomed to poverty, when they received new shoes, they saved them and continued to wear their old shoes until they became utterly unwearable. It was a joy for me to see them running, laughing, and wrestling.

I noticed other areas where I could help.

I saw the children in their classrooms writing on dark, coarse paper with pencil stubs about two inches long with very little graphite remaining. Students would lick their pencil stubs to find the slightest bit of graphite left. I sent notebooks, pencils, blackboards, chalk, and other school supplies to each classroom.

The children began to recognize me. They had been seeing me since their infancies. As I became more familiar with them, they would run to me and jump in a circle to touch me when I arrived. Then, when I left, they all tried to hold my hands and would plead, "Grandpa, don't go. Why do you have to go? When are you coming back?"

I would hug them and say goodbye, then walk away without looking back. I did not want them to see the tears running down my cheeks. I would hear them, though, in loud voices. "Goodbye, Grandpa. Goodbye, Grandpa."

CHAPTER THIRTY-SEVEN

The Children Come First

Kyuhee understood our priorities and knew what came first, despite any inconvenience my travel to North Korea caused us. Taking care of the orphans was our priority.

Appalled and profoundly saddened at how the famine had affected so many children, I built bread factories in Haeryong, Chongjin, and Buryong to provide lunch for the children at orphanages, local kindergartens, and public schools. We made round, fluffy buns, each weighing about an ounce and a half.

I used long holiday weekends in the United States for my trips to visit the orphans. Kyuhee would pack my bags right before Thanksgiving. "It is time for you to go to the children," she would tell me.

Thoughts of Kyuhee and the boys having turkey dinner without me made for a long journey. In a stretch of seven years, I missed turkey dinner at home.

Kyuhee's commitment to helping the orphans was as deep as mine, and she would often accompany me to meet the orphans and farmers and walk with me to the places I frequently visited.

Kyuhee and I worked together to improve mixing and steaming the dough of the buns. Kyuhee suggested adding salt to make the buns fluffier and tastier. She enjoyed the experience, and she felt her presence at the factories made her arduous trip worthwhile.

Women workers at the bread factories were delighted to see a person from America dressed humbly and working with them as if she was one of them. I saw the women had their ways of liking each other rather quickly.

On one trip, Kyuhee went with me to all three bread factories, and after tasting the buns, she suggested adding ingredients such as red beans or sweet fruit fillings to make them more enticing. We thought about adding sugar and fillings and analyzed costs. It became clear the expense of adding the extra ingredients would mean we could produce only half the number of life-sustaining buns we were distributing.

The question arose: Fewer but tastier buns? The answer came quickly and emphatically: More buns.

"We will make the buns tastier as soon as we get the farms to produce more fruit and deliver them to the factories," I said to Kyuhee.

Volunteers would deliver the buns by bicycle, carrying them in straw sacks as they pedaled to schools and orphanages. I recognized the need for a more efficient delivery system to bring the buns to more locations while still warm.

I bought an old van for the Buryong bread factory and asked the government to issue coupons for gasoline to defray expenses.

ဆ

I soon noticed something quite striking. While I was fulfilling many needs with the various goods I was sending, I could not bring their mother's love to the orphans or fill the emptiness in their hearts.

There were 1,600 students, 800 each from ages eight to fourteen, who attended two junior high schools in Chongjin and Kilju. Those kids were my age when I left Haeryong. Most were orphans who had grown up in circumstances like mine.

When I first saw those boys and girls, they were skinny, malnourished, and living in dire poverty. Their blank faces had no expression as they looked at me. I wondered what was in their minds.

They reminded me of myself when I was their age. I flashed back to the horrific days when I made the arduous trek with my family to Busan.

The difference between those orphans and me was that I always had my mother's uninterrupted love and care despite my family's hardships. I remembered my mother's warmth as she covered me with her body during the cold nights on our journey south. I felt that these children missed their mother's love.

I could not think of a way to comfort them.

Walking by a classroom one day, I heard music. I stopped and saw boys and girls playing a few old violins. I asked the music teacher if I could send them some instruments. She was exuberant and shouted, "Yes!"

We sent seven violins, ten accordions, four trumpets, a drum, and a sound system for the large hall where they practiced and performed. The teachers selected musically talented students and taught them how to play each instrument. I could only imagine the bursting joy and excitement of the students who were chosen to play.

The school invited me to a concert one day, which coincidentally was my birthday. I listened attentively as they played a Korean folk song, "Arirang." Its sweet melody brought me back to the days when I was their age, catching small crabs under rocks in the Tumen River, swimming with friends, and going to a Chinese shop at the edge of town to eat steaming white buns. I also thought about Akiko, my Japanese friend, the general's daughter.

After the concert, the school's principal took me to the playground, where eight hundred boys and girls wearing new winter jackets, pants, sweaters, and shoes lined up to greet me. To my surprise, they bowed and suddenly rose in unison, shooting their hands skyward, shouting, "Thank you, comrade Grandpa."

"I want you all to thank comrade Grandma, who loves you from far away and who made it all possible," I shouted back. I was on cloud nine, seeing and hearing eight hundred happy grandchildren thanking me. I wished Kyuhee had been there with me to share the moment.

⟡

One day, a teacher told me that some children broke their lunchtime bun in half and hid it to bring home to their hungry parents. I began to think about how I could help prevent such a wrenching scene. The only solution that came to my mind was to improve agricultural production.

I went to a nearby farm and walked up a hill where I could see hundreds of farmers working. "I must learn and teach them how to increase the rice and corn harvest," I said to myself. I prayed to God to give me the wisdom and courage to start an agricultural revolution.

I *promised* Kyuhee, I would not let a child feel he had to tear his small bun in half to feed his parents.

CHAPTER THIRTY-EIGHT

An Agricultural Revolution

The worst years of the devastating famine in North Korea lasted from 1996 through 1998.

Haeryong's unforgiving colder climate and poor soil conditions allowed farmers a very limited two-week window in April to seed rice, a crop crucial to survival. Everything they needed was in short supply or nonexistent, unthinkable challenges for the farmers.

They would plant rice seeds in graded soil at the corner of a plot, 1/36 of about three thousand square feet, then cover the area with polyethylene sheets until the seeds germinated. Those sheets were vital for growth during the crucial seeding process.

The plastic film retains moisture and attracts infrared rays from sunlight to keep seeds and soil warm and weeds out during the growing process. Without the sheets, the resulting rice stalks would be stunted and the rice softer and inferior.

Once the seeds germinated, farmers would then transplant the rice by hand into the paddies. It was labor-intensive work, but lives depended on it.

On one of my trips to Haeryong, I spoke to my guide, comrade Cho, about my expertise with plastic film sheets and bags back home. He quickly contacted the Overseas Compatriot Ministry in Pyongyang, which issued me a temporary entry permit to visit cooperative farms deep in the country's northeast.

Cho brought me to meet farmers, and I heard and saw firsthand their desperate need for agricultural film sheeting. Those visits allowed me to see and learn about rice production, and I began to think about the way to increase it.

I stopped in Yanji, China, and reached out to local agricultural experts on my way back home. I learned from them five essentials crucial to increasing rice production.

Farmers needed good, healthy seeds (1) and suitable chemical fertilizers for the type of soil in the area (2). In addition, they required agricultural film, mulch film, greenhouses (3), and mall reservoirs near the paddies (4). But, above all, the essential thing they needed was the proper training and know-how to put everything into place (5).

The experts I met convinced me that cooperative farms around Haeryong could double or perhaps even triple rice and corn production if I could persuade them to adopt those essentials. I knew it would not be easy. I believed any revolution would demand courage and the promised results were worth accepting new methods and the risks that went with them. I had to convince farmers to give up their traditional ways and accept new initiatives.

While the North Korean government controlled the distribution of the harvests, it did not provide resources such as seeds, fertilizer, farming tools, or the material to build reservoirs. Cooperatives simply followed the government's directions and had no freedom to change their farming practices. Furthermore, the farmers were afraid of not meeting the government's goals for each year's harvest.

North Korean farmers had been following traditional practices for generations. I found out getting them to try new methods, as I expected, was challenging.

At first, I could not understand why the farmers were reluctant to follow what I felt were compelling recommendations, especially when I was offering them for free.

Later, I grasped a fact, understandable, that farmers would not see the results of the new practices until the end of the entire lengthy growing process. They would have to wait until harvest. And the farmers were afraid that they would not be able to recover if the results of the new initiatives were below their standards or expectations.

I asked them to consider these new methods seriously, and I promised them I would compensate them for any shortfalls if my suggested changes did not work. I also had Pyongyang direct them to accept my recommendations.

In 1999, I built a company in Tumen City, a duplicate of my factory in Tamaqua, to produce plastic bags to supplement the parent company's overwhelming sales demand. Inside of me, perhaps, the real reason was I wanted to produce agricultural and mulch films for the Ham Kyung Book-Do province, the northeastern portion of North Korea, which held 20 percent of the country's population.

A farming revolution started in 1998. It was gratifying to start the fire.

I began to supply all the essential items and hired farming experts from Yanji to teach the new farming methods. Two experts lived at the cooperative farm for two years and worked around the clock, instructing farmers from germinating seeds through to harvest.

Townspeople, men and women, brought sickles and shovels to the hills and built small ponds to trap water from the foothills and channel it to the fields to flood the paddies.

I supplied four truckloads of the agricultural film—thousands of rolls weighing a total of eighty metric tons—each marked with the label, "A Gift from Joon Bai, native son from America," and printed instructions on how to use it.

The results were astounding. The following year, the rice harvest was quadruple the results of anything produced in recent years.

I also sent twenty metric tons of mulch film for growing corn. Again, the result was even more extraordinary, about five times that of any previous harvest, depending on locations.

Using the mulch film had a significant impact on vegetable growth as well. For vegetables such as turnips and potatoes, the mulch film had a considerable effect on its growth. Greenhouses would be the best, although they are costly to build.

We developed a new method of building a greenhouse. Instead of creating a self-standing structure, we carved into a hill, which made it part of the structure, then attached the rest of the greenhouse to it. Using the earthen wall made the greenhouse more robust, able to withstand strong wind, and importantly, cheaper to build. The cover on the roof, a film with an ultraviolet inhibitor, could be used for multiple years, needing to be replaced only every third or fourth year.

It was an innovation.

Growing cucumbers and tomatoes in greenhouses tripled and quadrupled the production. I became convinced of the tremendous benefits of using greenhouses for year-round production of rice and vegetables. Rice seeds germinated in those ideal conditions produced healthy and firm roots that withstood the northeast's cold air and steady winds. They were, then, hardy and ready to be transplanted outside. The farmers were happy and excited with the tremendous success.

In 1999, I shipped four truckloads of agricultural film and two truckloads of mulch film to a dozen cooperative farms in Chongjin and Haeryong. As a result, the rice production that year increased from two to five metric tons per hectare, and the corn harvest increase went from four to eight. Both crop harvests broke annual records that had been kept for decades.

To emphasize my point and remove any doubt about the new practices, I had each cooperative farm office hang two ears of corn, side by side. One represented the old methods, the other the new. The ear grown under mulch film was more than twice the size of the other.

Harvests increased even more in the third and fourth years, averaging seven metric tons of rice and twelve corn per hectare. At one greenhouse, a cucumber was so large, Kyuhee struggled to hold it. She said to me, "Joon, you could be a farmer. I don't mind being a wife of a farmer."

After seeing the incredible results of greenhouse farming, I began to believe we could improve the food situation in my hometown and perhaps the entire province.

It was a miracle, I felt, that only comes with God's blessings.

CHAPTER THIRTY-NINE

The Glorious Gift of Faith

Young Boon Ji cooperative farm, located by the ocean near Chongjin, was not ideal for growing corn because of the soil, ocean sands, and the cold weather. It produced a half-ton per hectare in its best year. In 2000, its director, Song Soon A, accepted my suggestion to use mulch film and proper fertilizer and to work with the experts I had brought in.

In 2001, her farm produced thirteen tons of corn per hectare, the most in North Korea, breaking a record. The central party awarded her a medal of achievement and promoted her to a high position in the Ham Kyung Book-Do Provincial Communist Party.

One day, she treated me and some of her farmers to a sumptuous lunch under pine trees at a seaside park. She told us that her farmers volunteered to get up before sunrise to catch crabs and abalone for the occasion, to express their appreciation to me. We drank some robust local wines and danced to accordion music.

I watched as farmers danced without a partner, each expressing joy in his or her style, like the Greeks I had seen during our travel to the Greek islands. They sang patriotic songs dedicated to North

Korea's leaders. And then, we all sang traditional folk songs expressing our love for our country. I saw their deep love for their county, always called their mother.

They all volunteered to sing songs dedicated to their mother. And I saw how much they loved their country.

〜

I frequently visited the cooperative farms to check that farmers were using the films correctly and to follow their progress. One night, after a long day's work, we sat to begin our dinner. Someone asked me to pray, saying, "Comrade Bai, we understand that you are a Christian, and that Christians pray before meals. So, please, do not mind us and go ahead and pray if you will."

I saw on the faces of everyone at the table that they echoed the request, and I felt the occasion was an excellent opportunity to speak of my belief in Christianity. I thought they wanted to hear what religion means and why people living in other countries believe in God.

So, I prayed.

"God, help us to care for our young children and allow us to succeed in our farming. I pray that you look after the safety and well-being of everyone in Haeryong and my family in America. I pray that our beloved country is unified and becomes one. I believe in peace and eternal life through you, God. I love you, God, with all my heart, soul, and mind. God, bless us all. I pray in the name of Jesus Christ."

I looked around the table and saw them looking like young children who had just listened to a fairytale. They did not quite understand the meaning of the faith I had spoken about, but they seemed to be envious of my belief in God.

〜

In 1998, I had met a Christian minister, a man named Choi, at Shenyang airport in China while waiting for the next flight to Pyongyang.

He told me he was a professor at Yanji University who taught animal science. He had many years of experience raising goats, he told me.

He said that goats are excellent livestock for farmers because they can sustain themselves almost anywhere, produce milk, and provide meat. A bonus, he said, was that goats are highly fertile and fit nicely into agricultural life in small farm towns like the ones I was helping in North Korea.

I bought one hundred goats for a farm near Rajin, North Korea. The following year, I visited the farm to see how things were. The shepherds told me all one hundred goats died of some type of disease they could not identify. I could not but suspect that they ate them all.

Many international media reported that three million North Koreans died of famine during that period, 1964 to 1968. The *New York Times*, Wikipedia, and Wilson Center all reported, "North Korea says that 240,000 people died in the four-year period. Outside the country, estimates range from 1.5 million to 3.5 million."

⌒

Going from place to place in northeastern North Korea, I often saw in the early evening or even after darkness fell, rain or not, people walking along country roads in dark-colored dresses, carrying backpacks of sewn-together cloth patches. "Where were they going, and how far did they have to go?" I wondered.

On one occasion, I asked the driver to stop the car to give a bottle of water to a man trudging along the edge of a dirt road with a boy. As I walked toward the man and attempted to hand over the bottle, he refused to accept it. He looked startled and could not believe a stranger would give him a bottle of water.

I set the bottle down in front of him, got back in the car, and began to drive off. In the rear-view mirror, I watched the man pick up the bottle in a cloud of dust. "The poorer you are, the greater your pride, particularly North Koreans," I thought.

~

People I saw on the road as I passed by appeared to have nothing to do and no place to go as they sat under swirling clouds of dust raised by passing cars. I wondered why they were sitting there. Could it be, perhaps, they had nothing to do at home?

Some faces were mottled and red, a sign, I was informed, that death was imminent. Maybe they sat by the road to be visible as they died from the famine—to not be alone in their final moments. I questioned why people had to die of starvation with all that God gives us in abundance.

~

Driving country roads anywhere in North Korea was dangerous, particularly in the Haeryong and Chongjin area, where narrow roads ran through high mountain passes. The roads covered with dirt and gravel had no guardrails to prevent a car from precipitous and fatal drops off the edge. I was in cars on several occasions when we nearly slid off the road.

One late November afternoon, my team of four left Haeryong headed for the Unification Bridge and, for me, to Tumen-Yanji-Seoul and home in California. Crawling up a steep slope before the road began to descend to Nam-Yang, it started to snow.

Our Toyota, with no snow tires, became mired, unable to move ahead, halfway up the slope. We had not thought to bring a snow shovel. The snowfall picked up as the sun disappeared quickly into the dark clouds. We tried pushing and rocking the car, but nothing worked. We were stuck.

We had only a handful of unroasted peanuts in a Ziploc bag and two bottles of soju, Korean rice wine, if we had to survive our precarious situation. We were fifty miles from civilization, trapped on a mountain with no means to call or signal for help.

For the first time in my life, I prayed to God for my own life.

When I looked up at the clouded sky, I heard the prayers of my mother and Kyuhee. A long hour passed, then the sun broke through the clouds. The warm sunlight began to melt the snow. The prayers of my mother and Kyuhee had worked.

We arrived at Nam-Yang two hours later. Soon after I crossed Unification Bridge and arrived Chinese side, the sky darkened again, winds picked up, and it began once more to snow heavily. I knew that on the mountaintop we had just left, the snowfall would be much heavier. I thanked God for protecting my team and me and allowing us to continue with our mission.

We had accomplished our objectives and had taught the farmers how to achieve good results. We had convinced them of the merits of the new farming revolution.

As I followed North Korean farm production in the northeast for the next five years, I saw results that confirmed they had maintained a harvest of six tons of rice and eleven tons of corn per hectare—a new standard.

I did not want ever again to see a child have to tear a bun in half and sneak it home to feed his family.

With hardworking farmers in my hometown, two Chinese farm experts, and the unwavering support and help of Kyuhee, we had done what some said was impossible. We succeeded in sparking an agricultural revolution in the worst possible place.

I had done all I could to keep children in my hometown from dying of famine. God had blessed me.

CHAPTER FORTY

A Lifetime Dream

I was eight years old when I saw my first movie, a Russian film, a nature documentary in color, at my small hometown theater. I was mesmerized.

Later, in Busan, after my family's harrowing journey to the South, movies became a way to escape hardships for a young boy. As I grew older, films became a passion, and I began to dream of acting in, directing, and producing a movie one day.

I would visit North Korea thirty-six times in nine years, from 1997 until 2005 to deliver aid. Each travel, time seemed interminable. The flight from California to Incheon International Airport in Seoul took thirteen hours, followed by an overnight stay at the airport hotel, a two-hour flight to Yanji, China, and seemingly endless hours between the flights and clearing customs and immigration.

My many trips to North Korea gave me the opportunity to write a journal about my experiences with orphans, the farmers, their lives, and the land. I saw that Koreans from both North and South express the sorrow of "blood and tears" from heartbreaking separation and yearning for loved ones they had not seen since the country's division more than fifty years ago.

I saw the forced separation between loved ones as the most painful human experience. To fill the empty hours, I wrote. I wrote hopeful notes about Koreans' desires and dreams to be reunited with their loved ones someday.

I could not understand why the country was still divided, and why there was no hope for unification in the foreseeable future.

Today it remains unacceptable to me. Korea is the only country still divided by war—a war that has caused millions of human tragedies.

North Korea and the United States have not signed a peace treaty to this day.

It was impossible to gauge what most residents of Haeryong and surrounding towns felt. Often, I would hear them praise their leader, General Kim Jung Il, passionately, expressing their appreciation for what he had provided for them.

Ordinary citizens were not allowed to speak openly to strangers. I noticed they did not seem unhappy or discontented with their lives, even though they had no freedom.

I wondered if their silence was because they were isolated from the rest of the world for so long and were unaware of what they were missing. Was that the reason why I heard no one complain? Or did they keep silent because they knew no one cared to listen to them? Perhaps they might not want to say what was on their minds for fear that whatever they said would be taken as complaints against the system in which they lived.

In my journal, I wrote nostalgically of my early days in Haeryong. Those were childhood days spent playing fearlessly in the majestic mountain landscape in which my hometown lay. Those were days in Wonsan when I could sit by a sparkling waterfall or walk the shoreline pine groves or rest atop a boulder on the beach and enjoy the peace of the oncoming waves. When I described those times, I found myself peaceful.

Those were happy times for me.

I began to enjoy writing, and the journal became more interesting. My childhood dream of making a movie took hold, and I felt a burning desire to transform my journal into a screenplay. I kept writing for five years.

I knew I was the only person who could speak for the voiceless people of my hometown, whose emotional wounds were unhealed. I heard the pleas of my mother and Kyuhee, praying that I would write what I saw in North Korea so the world could hear the cry of those silent people for unification and peace.

As I wrote, I watched my tears drop on the white paper of my journal, smudging the words. I *promised* myself that I would deliver their message.

CHAPTER FORTY-ONE

A Dream Achieved

I knew nothing about making movies in North Korea other than the fact that its leaders were passionate about them. I would learn quickly the North Korean film industry was as vigorous and energetic as anything in the West. It lacked only the latest technology.

When I traveled to Pyongyang with James, I had the opportunity to visit the enormous government-built film complex sitting on the city's outskirts, complete with indoor and outdoor studios spread over hundreds of acres. Many North Korean films were meant to be viewed only by North Koreans and were used to indoctrinate residents on the wonders and heroism of its leadership.

I saw many sets in the film complex built like authentic villages that were used also to house hundreds of extras. In the complex, you could find replicas of Russian towns from the 1930s and 1940s, Japanese inns and police buildings, and Manchurian villages. In addition, there were several large warehouses to store costumes and props, including American and Japanese army uniforms, guns, and tanks for war films.

The sets were used to shoot a series of films covering various episodes in the life of the founding father, Kim Il Sung, during his resistance struggle against the Japanese Imperial Army as a guerrilla fighter in Manchuria from 1930 to 1945.

My mother and Kyuhee were terrific muses.

I finished my screenplay in 2005. My script for the movie, which I called *The Other Side of the Mountain*, told the story of two lovers brought together by the Korean War. Theirs is a fateful love affair.

The screenplay tells:

"In the small town of Chunam Ri, North Korea, a young nurse, Sun Ah, saves a wounded South Korean soldier, Il Kyu, left behind from a battle. His South Korean identity is unknown to her until he tells her he must return south to bring his mother to Chunam Ri.

With his promise to return, Sun Ah waits a lifetime for him.

Il Kyu tried every possible means to reunite with his love. It proved impossible because there were no diplomatic relations between the Netherlands, where he lived and practiced as a doctor, and North Korea. Years passed, and their youth slipped away, but their love for each did not fade.

Il Kyu learns through the Red Cross that Sun Ah has passed away. He at last gets an unexpected opportunity to come to Pyongyang, where he learns Sun Ah is alive and that she has fulfilled their promises during their separation to build a hospital and care for orphans.

Shortly after their reunion, she dies of pancreatic cancer.

Il Kyu searches out for Sun Ah in all the places where they shared their love, and at the top of a mountain, he calls, 'Sun Ah, Sun Ah.'

He tries to touch her soul and jumps from the top of a high cliff to his death, so his soul can join Sun Ah's."

The film ends with village elders finding Il Kyu's body at the bottom of the cliff.

My task had two obstacles.

First, I had to find out if North Korea would even consider the idea of an American producing a movie in their country based on his own script. If they did, I would need the approval of the Overseas Compatriot Ministry in Pyongyang, which oversees international business activities, propaganda, intelligence, tourism, and guides for foreign visitors.

I met with Kim Kyung Ho, a minister who often praised my work for the people in Haeryong. "Compatriot Kim, I wrote a screenplay hoping to make a movie in our country," I said to him, handing him a copy of my screenplay. "I would like you to read it and let me know your thoughts."

The next day, he told me that he was impressed by the story.

As I was leaving his office, he held my hands firmly and said in a deep voice, "Comrade Bai, I want you to produce a movie based on your screenplay in your homeland and honor our great leader and our people."

CHAPTER FORTY-TWO

Delicate Negotiations

Minister Kim had his office make copies of my handwritten screenplay and passed them with his letter of recommendation to Professor Lee Hae Chang, an Art and Science Department director and head of the screenplay association.

Lee called together a group of screenwriters and presented my script. I first met with Professor Lee and Kim Eun Ok, a young writer from Chongjin with a bright future, in a conference room at the Koryo Hotel. Eun Ok had graduated from Kim Il Sung University and had written several screenplays, all well received by critics.

She reminded me of my youngest sister, Jung Ok, who had died so long before in Go-Chon. Both had large and beautiful dark eyes. I immediately liked Eun Ok for the courteous and respectful way she spoke to me. She later told me her uncle was killed in 1950 during the Korean War, so the topic of my screenplay resonated with her.

In the conference room, we exchanged greetings and sat to discuss the script. At one point during the early stages of the discussion, Eun Ok's face turned red. With her body shaking, she repeatedly said, "There is no way our girl falls in love with a South Korean soldier." For her even to think of such an event was unimaginable.

We would exchange opinions of our differing ideologies deep into the night.

I tried to convince her that all Koreans were from the same bloodline, with the same surnames, who spoke the same language. I emphasized that Koreans are separated not by ethnic identities, as in the United States, or by class difference, as in the United Kingdom, or religious differences, as in the Middle East, but by the whims of foreign superpowers who had seen fit to divide Korea.

"We are all a family, separated by war," I said. I explained that three powerhouses, the United States, Britain, and Russia, had agreed to divide Korea in the closing days of the Second World War at a conference in Yalta.

In a stern voice, I pointed out that we should remember Germany's Hitler and Japan's Hirohito as the evil men who had started the war, killed tens of millions of innocent people, and left us with humankind's greatest tragedy, including the egregious separation of Korea.

Professor Lee, who had been mostly quiet throughout, finally spoke. "This is a story of two people in love. It can happen," he said. "It is the story of our people, who have been pained by the war and by the separation of loved ones. We all hope for the unification of our land, don't we? I respect comrade Bai's words in the script."

As we were going down the hotel's long escalator, Eun Ok took my hand and said, "Grandpa, let us make a great film to show to our brothers and sisters in the South that we want the unification of our beloved lands."

When I held her warm, tiny hand, I felt the same Korean blood coursing through us.

When we got down to the front door, I saw it was pitch dark outside, with no lights on in the street or the high-rise buildings due to the frequent power shortages that had kept the city in darkness for some time. It was two o'clock in the morning, and I grew concerned.

I hoped Eun Ok and the professor got home safely.

⌇

Between the excitement of the film discussion and jet lag, I could not fall asleep. I tossed in bed until I heard the street songs Pyongyang plays every morning at six o'clock that began emanating from the speaker in the street outside my window. I decided to take a walk.

I found myself on an underground walkway near the train station and passed by several women standing in a circle around a boy who appeared to be about five years old, sitting on a stairway step. He was devouring square, brown cookies, the sort that reminded me of the ones from GI rations I had eaten many years before. I knew he had to be very thirsty.

I dashed to my hotel room, three blocks away, to get a bottle of water for the boy. When I returned to the exact spot where he had been sitting only minutes before, I saw a woman sweeping the step.

"Where did the boy go?" I asked the woman.

"I did not see any boy sitting there," she said.

Another cleaning woman walked over and said the same thing. There was no boy. Walking back to the hotel in disbelief, I could not help but think the boy's mother had abandoned her son. The cleaning women were not telling the truth.

"A mother would only do that out of desperation," I thought, "because she had no way to feed him." I saw how shocked the boy had appeared, sitting on the stairway alone, not knowing where his mother was and if she would come back to him.

I began shaking with the same profound sadness that had overwhelmed me when I buried my sister, Jung Ok. I questioned once again why these things had to happen.

I will never forget the expressionless face of that boy, looking blankly, straight ahead, not knowing what was happening to him. I imagine he was taken away by city caretakers. The boy was my grandson's age.

I thought about my brother Carl, who wandered the city of Dae Jung sick and frail, knocking on doors to beg for food. I also thought of my brother Ben, squeezed on the deck of the *Meredith Victory* with thousands of other refugees, hungry and cold for days on a pitching sea.

As fraught with peril and hardships as their situations were, Carl and Ben knew their mother would be waiting for them with her love and attention. But what about the boy on the step? I think of him even today.

What I witnessed that morning was one of the worst tragedies of humankind.

CHAPTER FORTY-THREE

A Hard-Won Agreement

Any screenplay, no matter where it is written or for whom—Hollywood or North Korea—is subject to the approval of many different interests. There are always calls for compromise, discussion, and scrutiny before filming begins—if it begins at all. My screenplay for *The Other Side of the Mountain* was no exception.

The afternoon following my meeting with Professor Lee and Kim Eun Ok at the Koryo Hotel, I took the screenplay to four senior writers in their seventies and eighties and three young university students majoring in film.

I asked them to read the script and respond to me with their comments. A day later, they all said to me the script delivered a great message of love and unification. The young writers said the screenplay brought them to tears. "Comrade Bai, please, make it into a movie," they all said to me.

A committee of nine directors of the Art and Science Ministry, two of whom I could only suspect were the heads of the government's propaganda ministry, wanted to add an account of one of the Korean War's tragedies, the No Gun Ri incident.

In the early days of the war, on July 26, 1950, the US Seventh Army, First Cavalry Division, massacred four hundred refugees, mostly women, elders, and children, in the farm village of No Gun Ri near the Military Demarcation Line dividing Korea. Decades later, the tragedy was acknowledged by the Pentagon, the US Congress, and President Bill Clinton, who issued a statement declaring, "I deeply regret that Korean civilians lost their lives at No Gun Ri."

I did not want *The Other Side of the Mountain* to reflect a negative view of the United States, which had come to South Korea to liberate the country from the North Korean invasion, sacrificing tens of thousands of young sons and daughters. I believed the No Gun Ri story was irrelevant to my story, a tale of love between two ordinary people.

I refused the suggestion.

I had no doubt that some of the North Korean leaders, who reviewed the script, had ideological differences. They were influenced by the Marxist-Leninist system of communism growing up and had practiced it their entire lives. I was influenced, buoyed, and strengthened by the fifty years I had lived and thrived under American capitalism and freedom.

Our screenplay discussion stalled as neither side backed down.

I spent hours reading as much as I could find, including newspaper accounts, correspondent reports, and official government reports, to learn the truth about what had happened at No Gun Ri.

I would make five more trips to Pyongyang before we agreed on a final screenplay. In the end, we compromised on several issues. I accepted their demand to add the No Gun Ri story to *The Other Side of the Mountain*, and in return, they agreed to leave in my message of God's gift of eternal life, a Christian concept I believed was essential to the story. More importantly, I wanted to follow the *promises* I made to my mother.

The North Koreans expressed their appreciation for my work at the orphanages and the farms, and they noted that my obvious love for the North Korean people was the tipping point in our stalemate.

They gave their approval for the script, the first time in the history of North Korea that a non-Communist Party writer outside its very strict system could proceed, noting that my theme of unification played a big part in their decision. They permitted two scenes in the script that illustrated the ultimate love between two people that would continue in eternal life, a Christian lesson I wanted to impart.

In one scene, a monk tells a legend of a young woman whose lover, a warrior, battles the thirteenth-century Mongol invaders of the Goryeo Dynasty in what is now Korea. Before the warrior departs for the battle, the two lovers place on each other's fingers matching jade rings as they embrace as a promise of their undying love.

With the war over, the young woman sees her lover is not among the triumphant warriors returning home. His compatriots brought back only his helmet and jade ring. She puts his ring on her finger and jumps from the top of a waterfall to her death, rejoicing in her imminent reunion with her lover in heaven.

From that day, legend says, the water in the pond at the foot of the waterfall turned jade green from the sunlight reflecting on their rings.

The original ending of my screenplay would prompt another objection from the committee, and I agreed to change it. As I had written the conclusion, the South Korean solider Il Kyu jumps to his death from a cliff after learning his lover, the nurse, Sun Ah has died. The committee felt suicide was a dishonorable act. I rewrote the scene and had Kyu die of heart failure.

In the end, North Korean leaders felt their addition of the No Gun Ri incident achieved their propaganda objectives for the film, telling the world about the inhumane and what they considered "criminal" acts of American imperialists on innocent people in the small village.

Deep in my heart, I knew I had achieved more significant objectives.

Through my screenplay, I spread the message that love answers all human-made miseries and divisiveness, that death cannot separate it, and love can unite us. I wanted all Koreans to believe that we could unify our divided land with love. I tried to deliver the prayers of my mother and Kyuhee that guided my heart.

Eun Ok was invaluable for helping polish the screenplay, and since I had written it in English, for translating it. Other scriptwriters on our team helped as well. I considered the experience a privilege, and I was thrilled to make a movie in North Korea.

The Other Side of the Mountain would deliver my mother's wish that someday people in her homeland would receive God's blessing.

The *promise* I made to my mother and Kyuhee had started.

CHAPTER FORTY-FOUR

The Pieces Come Together

With the painstaking negotiations over the screenplay completed and approved, we were ready for the next step on the way to fulfilling one of my long-held dreams, making a movie. My first task was to choose a director.

I was excited to begin selecting key members of the production staff. The Ministry of Art and Science instructed the Korean Film Group to assemble a pool of possible candidates for director for my approval. I reviewed four strong candidates, studying their biographies, watching most of their previous work, and interviewing each. I wanted to pick one who possessed the sensitivity to absorb and express my story clearly and artistically.

I selected Jang In Hak, the final candidate I interviewed. Jang told me he developed a burning desire to work with me as soon as he read my screenplay. He had been captivated by my story of the ultimate love between two people, their sacrifices, and my script's more profound emphasis on values and life, he told me.

Among Jang's many highly acclaimed films was *The School Girl's Diary*, a moving film about the interactions between two teenage sisters, their parents, and a teacher who kept their family together after an unexpected tragedy. I thought Jang brought out the sensitivity and emotional flow of that simple story. He connected me to other key members of the production crew.

Jang introduced me to Han Yong Soo, a senior cameraman awarded the Great Leader's Medal of Excellence in cinematography. Jang also introduced me to composer Song Dong Hwan, considered the best in the business in Pyongyang. Song had also fallen in love with the screenplay and wanted to compose the original music and the soundtrack in its entirety. Song, a gifted musician, told me the melodies flew into his head as he read the script.

The recording studio near the Yanggakdo Hotel in Pyongyang, where most foreign visitors stay, is a round building with an umbrella-shaped roof that houses a dozen soundproof rooms. It has a sizable central auditorium wired for intricate recording, with hundreds of microphones to pick up the nuanced tones of the various instruments, as well as an impressive chorus of one hundred voices.

Song arranged for me to hear solo musicians playing the main songs with various instruments: guitar, violin, piano, flute, and gayageum (a twelve-string Korean instrument). Then he asked me to choose the instruments to play in the recording. He praised me for selecting a violin and Korean flute for one song, and a violin and guitar duet for another.

Song had his entire ensemble of instruments and a chorus of one hundred voices play two sections of the theme music just for me, allowing me to make suggestions before making the final recording for the film. Chorus members, all music students and young wives, made an enormous sacrifice to record the new works for the film.

One session was scheduled for Kimchee Day, a fall day that the entire country sets aside and devotes to making kimchee. A Korean staple, kimchee is a traditional side dish of salted and fermented vegetables, mainly cabbage, with a bit of radish and cucumber mixed with garlic, red pepper, and other dressings. Farmers deliver truckloads of cabbage to neighborhoods, where the community pitches in to make kimchee for the winter.

Chorus members could not afford to miss Kimchee Day because cabbage trucks come only once a season. But they all went to the studio to record the film's soundtrack. Their voices in *The Other Side of the Mountain* will live with the movie for many generations.

I was extremely pleased with the title songs and the soundtrack Song composed. It reminded me of the haunting and lovely music composed for David Lean's *Dr. Zhivago* by Maurice Jarre.

I quickly began to see that everyone involved was a tremendously talented musician, no matter their role. As the sessions continued, I would participate, often giving the musicians high fives after stunning performances. Song kept telling me how much he enjoyed my presence at the studio and that he appreciated my interests in his music.

At one recording session, I noticed a skinny young woman sitting on the floor in the corner of the sound room, her head down and legs crossed. I thought she was a studio cleaner taking a break. Song introduced me to Ms. Choi Young Ja, who would be the lead vocalist in the film.

Once again, I learned that there is no class difference in North Korean society. Everyone is treated equally regardless of their position, whether it is a janitor or the studio director.

Indeed, it was a pleasure and a joy for me to work with Song and his staff, and I treasured all the exciting moments we shared. Those were the joyful days of my life.

I hope I will have more opportunities to work with them again. I miss them.

CHAPTER FORTY-FIVE

The Final Step: Choosing the Actors

Finding our lead actress was a gift, like Billy Wyler finding an unknown Audrey Hepburn to play Princess Ann in *Roman Holiday*.

When I saw Kim Haen Sook's performance in a short television drama, I knew right away she was perfect to play the lead role of the village nurse in *The Other Side of the Mountain*. When I interviewed her in person, I saw a beautiful young woman who embodied strength, innocence, righteousness, and Korean femininity.

Finding the lead actor to play Il Kyu was not as easy.

At first, we asked four candidates to act a scene from the screenplay for us, with an actress reading the role of Sun Ah. After hours of evaluation, Jang and I agreed that none met our expectations. We asked two more actors to audition. The tall, good-looking, and young Kim Ryung Min played the role of Il Kyu with an innocence tempered by a strong sense of justice and firm conviction. We knew he was our lead actor.

For the role of the father of Sun Ah, a hunter, selecting the esteemed actor Shin Myung Ook, a winner of the Medal of Excellence from the Great Leader, was a snap. I knew he was perfect for the part from his earlier films.

181

Just for Kyuhee, Jang staged a theatrical performance with the leading and supporting actors to play two scenes, accompanied by background music on the studio stage. Kyuhee was impressed by it and praised Jang and his staff for their commitment to *The Other Side of the Mountain*.

"We thank Kyuhee mother for coming from so far away to cheer us and encourage us," Jang said to his entire crew. Using the term "mother" in an affectionate and respectful reference to Kyuhee showed how much he appreciated her. It was the North Korean way.

With what I thought were the major obstacles behind me, I felt we were close to scouting locations for the film and beginning actual shooting.

I was mistaken.

CHAPTER FORTY-SIX

A Necessary Delay

The script called for sensitive cinematography on a scale not yet seen in North Korea. We had the talent and vision to create a film, but we did not have the equipment. I insisted that *The Other Side of the Mountain* be filmed with synchronized sound, the first occasion it would be used in North Korean movie history.

The film studio had three non-sync ARRI camera bodies, each more than decades old, four heavily used lenses, and only a few obsolete pieces of lighting equipment. I quickly learned that a new synchronized ARRI camera body and three Zeiss lenses would cost over $400,000.

I was able to find a used AARI sync sound camera body for $65,000 through a used-equipment supplier, Alan Gordon Enterprise, in Hollywood. I bought three new Zeiss lenses and a dolly support rail for $155,000. With the savings from buying the used camera body, I purchased a new ARRI outdoor lighting system for $195,000.

That was not enough.

Cinematographers asked for indoor lighting equipment. I went again down to Los Angeles and purchased used tungsten daylight lamps. While I was there, I also bought a sound recorder, a handheld sound receiver, batteries, and other miscellaneous but necessary equipment such as monitors, filters, and two snowmaking machines.

The short trip south cost $160,000.

I would spend close to $600,000 for equipment essential to produce the movie my screenplay deserved, the very best tools to capture and deliver the message. I would also purchase a used bus and fuel for the studio and treat staff for an occasional meal while traveling to location shoots.

Purchasing the equipment was painless compared to shipping it to North Korea. US sanctions against North Korea and the size of packages permitted to be shipped by air required some nimbleness. Our freight forwarders packed goods in three pallets and shipped them to Hong Kong, where they would then be trans-shipped to Beijing and on to Pyongyang. Each item had to be cleared from the American sanctions by being classified as non-military items.

The shipment to Hong Kong and Beijing went without a hitch. However, the local custom forwarder held the pallets in Beijing because they were too large to fit the Koryo Airlines cargo space. As a result, everything had to be unpacked and then repacked into smaller packages, each requiring new permits and new insurance coverage.

It took six weeks for these vital shipments to arrive at the studio. Nonetheless, we were ready to begin the production at last. Or so I believed.

CHAPTER FORTY-SEVEN

Thoughts on Freedom

The unexpected shipping problems delayed a celebration the studio had planned to mark the first day of shooting in the presence of Kyuhee and me.

We were stranded in our hotel for two weeks waiting for the cameras to arrive. To pass the time, we played countless games of Sudoku; I found some of the difficult puzzles quite challenging. Not so for Kyuhee. I would have to turn to her for help, which she provided almost nonchalantly, so good was she at Sudoku.

She was the master of Sodoku.

Filling the empty hours because of the unexpected delays soon became tedious. I once again looked to Kyuhee for her calming presence. She never once complained.

We became bored and looked for things to do.

We were fascinated by daily street life. Pedestrians we would pass on our walks about Pyongyang all wore a Great Leader badge pinned to their jackets. Most seemed hurried, and all wore expressionless faces. On the city's immaculate streets, we saw women, toting large bundles on their heads, rushing to catch streetcars while holding their children's hands. At every major street crossing, we saw a young, pretty traffic director in blue uniform, blowing a whistle and guiding traffic, just a few cars at any time.

We noticed others pulling two-wheeled carts past walking young men reading books. We could see resilience and the will to survive on their dark and thin faces. Such scenes led us to think deeply about the value of freedom, and as Kyuhee and I often did, we talked about what we had seen in our world travels.

Sitting on a bench in a park near our Pyongyang hotel observing passersby, Kyuhee brought up our travels to the Soviet Union in 1990. Pyongyang looked very much like Leningrad at the time.

Leningrad, now St. Petersburg, was very poor when we visited. There, we saw soldiers wearing uncomfortable winter uniforms in the heat of summer and long lines of people waiting for streetcars. Our Leningrad hotel was a large and dull Soviet-style building with no shops, cafés, or bars.

Nevertheless, we thought Leningrad was perhaps one of the most beautiful cities in the world. The State Hermitage, the Peterhof in the Petrodvortsovy District, *and* Nevsky Prospect were among the city's treasures that impressed us.

We attended a performance of the opera *Faust* at the Leningrad Opera House. I found it captivating, with beautiful singing and dancing, but jet lag and the theater's comforting darkness put me to sleep during Act IV, despite Kyuhee's attempt to keep me awake. In an odd twist, they served sugar water, not champagne between acts.

The Soviet government did not permit foreign visitors to bring outside publications into Leningrad, especially the Bible or capitalist material. I had known that, and as we were leaving the Helsinki train station in Finland to start our trip to the Soviet Union, I pulled a *Time* magazine from my backpack and was about to toss it into a trash bin.

Kyuhee stopped me and asked me to bring it with us. She wanted someone, any Russian who read English, to pick it up and read about what was happening in the rest of the world. I kept the magazine with me and left it on a park bench near our hotel in Leningrad.

"Liberty is a paradigm of humanity, but excess freedom has turned our society into human rubbish," I told Kyuhee.

"I would rather not drink champagne," Kyuhee said and looked at me with sparkling eyes. "Can we have both? Can we drink champagne and not commit evil deeds?"

I quietly kidded her that our next destination could be a Siberian concentration camp if we got caught with *Time* magazine and were heard criticizing their communist system. I did not hear her response, but I knew she would say, "I am willing to trade my freedom for the freedom of all Russians."

I sensed that Kyuhee wanted to spread the ideals of freedom to oppressed Russians who did not know what freedom meant. She also wanted to tell them what was happening around the world.

Kyuhee and I felt Russians were exceptionally resilient and artistically gifted people.

Our guide told us that twenty-three million Russians died during World War II—eighteen million men and women, mostly young— leaving millions of mothers and grandmothers in deep sorrow.

She reminded us that millions of Russian women fought heroically through one of the coldest winters on record during the infamous Siege of Stalingrad to defeat Hitler's invading forces. That stand, in the end, would lead to the defeat of the Third Reich and help end World War II, the guide told us.

I saw Kyuhee turn and give the guide an enthusiastic thumbs up.

CHAPTER FORTY-EIGHT

A Sense of Fulfillment

With the delays continuing, Kyuhee and I returned home. We simply did not know how long it would take for the camera and other equipment to clear customs and make it to Pyongyang. After two weeks back home, I learned the camera was about to leave Beijing, finally.

I was excited to return to Pyongyang and about the prospect of finally beginning filming. I went to Pyongyang by myself this time because Kyuhee had other commitments, parent-teacher meetings, and church choir activities.

I usually stayed at the centrally located Koryo Hotel for its good breakfast and its convenient location, but this time, I chose Pyongyang Hotel by Dae Dong River that runs through the city along Kim Il Sung Square.

I continued to learn more about life in modern North Korea.

I went for a haircut. The barber informed me that I could choose from one of fourteen styles, all displayed in pictures posted on the wall in front of the barber chair. Furthermore, he told me that everyone was required to cut their hair in one of the styles shown.

I sensed that there was no room for non-conformity. I picked a style closest to my usual. While the barber worked, I glanced at the women's salon across the hallway and saw the picture of nineteen short women's styles, none falling to the shoulder.

༄

Each morning I walked alone, without a guide, on the street along the river to Kim Il Sung Square, for daily exercise. I was the only non-North Korean citizen walking on that vast square, often shown on television news reporting on events in North Korea, alone. On National Celebration days—the birthdays of founding father Kim Il Sung, General Kim Jun Il, Military Day, Communist Party Day, Independence Day, and National Day—hundreds of thousands of school children and military personnel parade along the street starting and ending at that square.

As I walked across the square, I saw a series of numbers marked on the concrete pavement identifying the spots where children were positioned before and after the lengthy parades. As I was standing on one spot, I thought back to the day, sixty years before, when I was twelve and had joined the Communist Party and paraded through that same space, starting from one of the thousands of designated spots.

It seemed like centuries ago.

I stared at the enormous portraits of Karl Marx and Vladimir Lenin at the top of the building towering to the left side of the square and at the Juche Tower across the Dae Dong River. Now I was on the verge of making an impact on the country of my birth with a film I had worked so hard to write and produce that would open hearts and minds. I thought of Kyuhee and our sons and our lives in America.

It had been a fulfilling journey.

CHAPTER FORTY-NINE

Scenes from a Movie

A good film is a tapestry woven from disparate yet moving scenes. The writer and director hope that the film's final brilliance will shine as a seamless story that draws viewers in, stirs their emotions, and commands their rapt attention. A good film will prompt its audience to leave the theater thrilled they have been fortunate to see it—and, its creators hope, to share its power later over coffee or drinks and to spread the word of its worth.

Making a movie requires vision. Its writer and director must work in harmony to shoot individual scenes they will assemble deftly in the editing room later. I had done my work with the writing. Everyone agreed I had the best director in North Korea to take my vision and use his skill to motivate the actors and the cinematographer to create what we hoped would be a stunning film.

No film is shot chronologically, that is, as the story unfolds onscreen for the viewers. Logistics and timing require that scenes be shot out of order, then blended during the editing process. It is up to the director and actors to imagine the story and summon their art to play their roles with passion and skill.

They did.

Waiting for the camera to arrive, Jang and I selected where we would film. We would use five separate locations: the studios in Pyongyang;

September Mountain near Pyongyang; Sinuiju, a city on the Yalu River bordering China; Kaesong, a town near the demilitarized zone; and Nampo, a port city in the western part of North Korea. The viewers of the final product did not know that each scene we filmed in *The Other Side of the Mountain* had its own story.

∽

After a successful opening ceremony, I noticed the makeup staff was working with what appeared to be outdated material while we shot a scene where Sun Ah treated a wounded soldier. I also saw they were not particularly skilled. I knew already the Pyongyang studio lacked the visual- and sound-effect tools of more advanced filmmaking countries. The makeup crew was even further behind.

Kyuhee and I went to Kryolan, a makeup supplier in downtown San Francisco. We purchased special-effect materials and a variety of makeup, such as tear sticks, eye blood, F/X blood, spirit gum, facial foundations, skin creams, imitation mustaches, and hairpieces.

It was unnerving to learn that the production staff used real guns, bullets, and explosives for the battle scenes. In one scene, a piece of flying glass from a bomb explosion cut Haen Sook's forehead to such an extent she needed a bandage, which had not been scripted. I rewrote the scene in a way where the bandage was not out of place, and we shot without interruption.

∽

Another scene called for an interrogator to repeatedly throw Ryong Min to a jail cell's concrete floor. Again, there was nothing like a fake mattress, soft landing pad, or a stuntman available to soften his falls. After four takes of the scene, Ryong Min's knees and elbows were bruised and bloody. I noticed Haen Sook rush to him, clean his wounds, and put on a bandage. Such injuries forced us to change the shooting schedule often.

⌇

In one scene, I wanted a rat to crawl on a tin plate of corn a prison guard places in front of Il Kyu, who sits on the concrete floor in the corner of a jail cell. As I was preparing to return home for a break, I stressed to Jang how vital this scene was. He assured me that he would get it done.

Jang's neighbors found three giant rats. With the lights on and the camera rolling, they let one rat loose from its cage. The frightened rat scurried around the set but did not approach the plate. Jang did not feed the second rat for five days, thinking it would rush to the plate and eat the corn. With the lights on and the camera rolling, they released the second rat. The rat barely moved toward the plate then suddenly dropped dead. They starved the third rat for three days.

It succeeded.

⌇

We used real explosives to blow up an old bridge straddling the Kaesong River that had been damaged years before during the war. At the sound of the huge and successful explosion, we all clapped our hands, shouting, "No fake in this scene."

⌇

Our leading actors, Ryong Min and Haen Sook, fell in love during the filming.

None of the actors or any of the film crew noticed what was happening. An old fox that I am, I knew something was going on between them during the shooting of the jail scene where Ryong Min got hurt. I saw her hands shaking as she cleaned his wounds. Later, I noticed them sitting on a flat rock having lunch, giggling, and looking at each other with eyes full of love.

I knew what was going on. For proof, I took a few pictures and showed them. The couple told me later they sensed I knew they were in love. Only the three of us knew. The rest of the crew was oblivious. Their genuine love brought chemistry to their scenes.

They got married toward the end of the filming, though I could not attend because of a scheduling conflict. When I returned to Pyongyang, the two newlyweds invited me to a lovely traditional Korean restaurant and bowed to me, as couples do to their parents on such an occasion.

They had a baby girl named Jin Hae, who is seven years old now. Jin Hae often writes to me, asking, "Dear Grandfather, I miss you. When are you coming to see us?" I tell my friends, "I produced a great movie, everyone said, but there is nothing that comes close to producing a family."

∽

I insisted we shoot most of the outdoor scenes in natural snow and use snowmaking machines for indoor settings with an outdoor scene as a backdrop only if we had to. We had to wait for a few weeks for snowfall, but it was worth it.

We were lucky to have a heavy, fresh snowfall the night before one shooting, allowing us to film several scenes, including a wrenching one of the lovers' separation. The cinematographer, Han, Jang, and I agreed there would be no need for a re-shoot. We all wanted to leave our fresh footsteps in the snow.

∽

During location shoots, on special occasions such as the Great Leader's birthday, I provided food for the actors and crew, usually rice balls, fried chicken, dry fish, and kimchee.

In daily North Korean life, the government distributes equal food rations and pays its people the same small salary. The amount of food in a ration is determined by family size, the number of adults and children by age, and the type of job each family member performs. For example, a man who works at a heavy-duty job gets a few grams more rice than a clerk employed in an office.

〜

During a shoot on September Mountain, Jang, the cinematographer, the art director, and I were about to open the bento lunch boxes I had brought from my hotel. We sat comfortably on a flat rock Jang had chosen beside a waterfall. A skinny young soldier approached us and asked if we could leave him any leftovers.

Jang, an ex-mxarine, shouted at him. "How dare you bother elders having a meal."

The soldier was apologetic and said, "I am sorry, Sir, but I have not had anything to eat since yesterday."

Jang told him to come back in half an hour.

Seeing the soldier walking away from us in his loose uniform, I remembered the time fifty years before on my family's long trek to Busan when I had picked up the maggot-infested corned beef in a can.

I sensed my three companions' shame for their young soldier exposing this sad state of North Korean affairs in front of me. I could also sense none of us would finish our lunch. I left half of my own, telling the others that I had a big breakfast.

When the soldier returned, we gave him my bento filled with a few more bites from the others. The young soldier flashed a big smile, snapped a salute, and looked at Jang.

"Sir, I truly appreciate your generosity. I will share this food with a compatriot in my unit," he said.

We relaxed and began to talk about the afternoon's work. A few minutes later, the soldier approached again. "Sir, may I have your leftover cigarettes?"

We all laughed.

Jang gave him what was in his pocket.

Kyuhee often traveled with me to the Pyongyang studio and the locations. She was there for a scene in which Sun Ah treats wounded soldiers. Standing by the camera and knowing Kyuhee was a nurse, Jang, asked her to show the actress playing Sun Ah how to clean and treat wounds, which Kyuhee did with meticulous care.

Jang thanked Kyuhee in front of the camera crew. Kyuhee bowed her head in the direction of Jang and to the crew to acknowledge them with her sweet smile.

〜

The government had left intact a temple, built hundreds of years before, to preserve the history of Buddhism. The night before shooting at the temple, Jang asked eight actors and crew members to bring one dish each for lunch to celebrate the seventieth birthday of comrade Han, the director of cinematography. Jang hoped the occasion would deepen the burgeoning friendship we were developing.

At lunch, we squeezed ourselves into a small room and sat in a circle. The elderly head monk brought rice wine in a large, impressive ceramic jug, telling us it was more than one hundred years old and brought out only for special occasions.

Each one opened his lunch box, one at a time, revealing a spread of modest dishes of cabbage kimchee, steamed eggs, cucumber kimchee, sesame fried rice, a small fish, Do Ru Muck, and yet another radish kimchee and vegetables. Seeing the display, the best they could bring for a special occasion, I could tell how poor they were.

We all bowed to Han and wished him long life, then drank the wine in wooden cups. "I have sipped some good rice wines in Kyoto and Seoul, but this wine is the best I have tasted," I told everyone to much applause. We then took turns telling jokes and laughing. It was an extraordinary experience for me to see them express themselves with such genuine respect and courtesy in honesty.

I posed a question. "Is there divorce or murder or suicide in your cities?"

"No, none," they said in loud voice in chorus. Then, added, "Perhaps, a tiny percentage of divorce, but no homicide or suicide."

These were people who had grown up under a strict socialist ideology, loving their mothers, being kind to each other, and dedicating themselves to their country. I wondered if evil had room to squeeze into their society. I have heard people say, "Humans are evil by nature." I wondered. Would it be better for them not to have champagne?

Evil had minimal impact on their lives because evil acts could not provide them with better lives or higher positions. They did not understand the intricacy of evil deeds. To them, evil was the Japanese imperialist who treated them as inferior—lesser humans.

Kyuhee once asked me, "Joon, can we have freedom and practice the virtues of what freedom brings?" at the park bench in Pyongyang. She answered her question. "Yes. It is God's command."

It was the most enjoyable lunch I have had in my life, for it was not the taste of food but the taste of friendship, a time with friends, lesser evil.

∽

Many scenes were shot at the top of September Mountain during the winter to capture its picturesque winter wonderland, with snow capping the colorful landscape surrounded by magnificent frozen waterfalls. A few scenes demanded precision, with only a few seconds available for the camera to capture the sun peeking out from behind the mountain to expose the luxuriant beauty.

September Mountain was a four-hour drive away from Pyongyang. There were no hotels or inns, only a few farmhouses. Jang asked the crew and actors to stay overnight in small groups at the farmers' houses. The following morning, just before sunrise, they all arrived at the location site, bringing hot potatoes and corn in their pockets to keep them warm.

That was their breakfast.

When I saw the cast and crew working in such challenging environments, with enormous passion and dedication to deliver my story to the screen for all to see, I felt privileged, not as a screenwriter or producer, but as a genuine member of that group.

They all approached me individually to say that they felt privileged to be part of making *The Other Side of the Mountain*. Some held my hands and said that they would do their best to make it a great film. The senior actor, Shin Myung Ook, shook my hand and looked into my eyes. "Comrade Bai, it is a great honor to play a part in your wonderful script," he told me.

∽

After a long day of shooting, as the actors and crew sat, relaxing, I told them, "I believe I was born to make this movie, and I would like you to feel the same. Let us show the world that we can make a great film."

They all raised their fists and looked at me, and said enthusiastically in loud voices, "I am with you. Let us make the greatest film."

Later, after a night of shooting, we sat around a bonfire chatting about the scene scheduled for the following day. The dark blue sky was filled with millions of bright stars that felt so close we could touch them.

One of the supporting actresses, just out of university, asked me, "Comrade Grandpa, do you think one day our brothers and sisters in the South will see this film?"

"Yes, they will, I promise," I told her. It was, for me, a *promise* of a lifetime.

I hoped *The Other Side of the Mountain* sent a message to Koreans, North and South, that love can endure the tragedy. My mother's love exemplified this belief.

I dedicated the movie to my beloved mother.

CHAPTER FIFTY

The Premiere

May 15, 2012, an exuberant and triumphant day I had long dreamed of, finally arrived.

I was filled with enormous pride as I sat in a grand chair reserved in memory of the Great Leader, Kim Il Sung, at the Mo Ran Gan Theater, Pyongyang's grandest, for the premiere of *The Other Side of the Mountain*.

The emotional event would be the first of many showings at film festivals around the world that produced the same heartening results—tears and hope for the unification of Korea.

That day in Pyongyang was also overwhelmingly bittersweet. I sat alone, without the driving force that had brought me there, who had inspired me all those years to write and produce the film.

Kyuhee had begun to lose her ability to manage her everyday activities. Pyongyang was too far from her doctors and hospital.

I traveled to Pyongyang myself.

As I left, I kissed Kyuhee a heartfelt goodbye at the door as she struggled to stand from her wheelchair. "I don't want you to worry about me, Joon," she told me. "Please have a successful festival. Tell Director Jang and the actors and crew I miss them."

I observed a sea of Pyongyang men dressed in formal suits and ties and women wearing vibrantly colorful traditional Korean two-piece dresses, a slimming top with a long-sleeved jacket, and graceful full-bottom skirts. As I watched in awe, they seemed to be floating through the air.

High-ranking government officials in Mao suits occupied the theater's front seats. Behind them, the theater was filled to capacity. The Minister of Art and Science, comrade Kim Young Sam, introduced me to the audience and spoke briefly about making the film. He praised my humanitarian efforts in Great Leader Kim Jong Il's mother's birthplace and my dedication to promoting the party's mission, unification.

I stood and spoke of my joy at making a film in my home country and how much I appreciated the warmth extended by citizens of every town I visited. I also thanked the Party, Ministry, studio staff, production crew, and actors for their efforts. I added a special thanks to the Great Leader for his interest in *The Other Side of the Mountain* and for making it possible to produce the film.

After the final scene of the cast singing the unification song on the slope of September Mountain and the reunions of the separated families, the theater lights came on.

Everyone stood, turned to me, and applauded enthusiastically for what seemed like ten minutes.

Then, finally, I stood in response, raised my fist, and shouted, "Let us all work together toward the unification of our beloved land."

The entire audience, still facing me, raised their fists in unison, and in a single roaring voice, replied in kind. "Unification, unification," they shouted, many with tears running down their cheeks. On their sad but hopeful faces, I could see their seventy years of yearning for the reunion of their families and the unification of their country.

I looked to my right for Kyuhee. I wanted her with me to share the moment.

As we walked out of the theater, Minister Kim Young Sam turned to me and said, "Comrade Bai, how did you do it?"

"I simply shook the tree," I told him. "It was possible because of the passion and dedication of Director, the actors, and the production crew, and the enormous support of others, including extras, farmers, and ordinary citizens."

"Compatriot Bai, your film will rank as the greatest film in our nation's movie history. We are proud of you for your achievement," he replied, adding, "you are our big brother who happens to live in a country far away. But you will always be with us."

In 2013, Minister Kim wrote me that each citizen in North Korea had watched *The Other Side of the Mountain* in theaters and on television more than three times. He added that the film would be kept in the republic's archives for future generations to savor. Then he shocked me, quite pleasantly, by saying in his official letter that the studio plans to build a statue in my honor in front of its central plaza near the main studio.

Recently, I had dinner at a North Korean-run restaurant in Yanji, China. The waitresses found out who I was, came to my table, and asked if they could take a photo with me. They told me they had seen the movie several times, and then they sang the title song and recited dialogue from the film.

In the intervening years since the North Korean premiere, I was busy spreading the word worldwide.

CHAPTER FIFTY-ONE

Hawaiian World Premiere

"I succeeded in reaching half of Korea, but there is more to do," I told Kyuhee. "I need to bring the film to the other half of Korea, America, and people everywhere in the world."

The Other Side of the Mountain's world premiere was at the Hawaii International Film Festival at Dole Cannery theater in Honolulu on October 17 and 22, 2012. Sadly, Kyuhee could not attend.

I traveled to Honolulu three days before the start of the festival. Kyuhee and I had visited Hawaii many times before, but this time, as I walked along a wave-swept beach before the first showing, I felt empty. I wanted Kyuhee beside me. I wanted to hold her hand as we had done on such walks so many times before.

With my good friend Barry Jay, a local Hawaiian, and my business partner in the past, we stopped at every Korean church, mini-store, and beauty salon we could find to hand out fliers. We greeted shop owners and asked if we could put posters on their doors and windows. All welcomed us kindly and asked us to leave fliers for their friends.

It took three days for us to cover Honolulu's streets under the island's hot afternoon sun. I had live interviews with local ABC TV affiliate KGMB's *Sunrise; Hawaii Morning Live Now* and two Korean radio stations. I was elated to learn from the theater that the showings were sold out.

It was, I thought, a clear indication that *The Other Side of the Mountain* was making an impact. The enthusiastic reception for a film made in North Korea enhanced my belief that people from every background wished to see my movie.

At the first screening, I shook with emotion and excitement as I stood on the stage. I could neither talk nor hold back my tears in front of more than 250 people. The faces of my friends back in Pyongyang who worked all those years with me flashed before my eyes—the faces of Jang, Haen Sook, Ryung Min, Han, and the others. I thought back to my long journey as I stood there, unable to speak.

My mother's inspiration and Kyuhee's prayers filled my heart. I was frozen. I knew I could not just stand there and cry. I handed the microphone back to the program manager, Anderson Le, who had introduced me. He embraced me and pushed me back to the stage. "Mr. Bai, it's okay. The audience is waiting to hear from you," he told me.

I gathered myself and spoke of how happy I was to show *The Other Side of the Mountain* to the Hawaiian people for the first time. Then I added my genuine feelings. "I could not pick a better city for my film's world premiere," I said. "I wish my friends in North Korea were here with me tonight," I added, wiping the tears flowing down my face.

I wished my dear Kyuhee was there standing next to me. I knew she would squeeze my hand with all the strength she had, then tell me, "Joon, I am proud of you."

After the showing and a question and answer session, I stood at the exit and shook hands with people as they departed. Each expressed how impressed they were with the cinematography, the acting, the music, the scenery, and the moving love story. Some told me they had not known that North Koreans wanted unification.

At the end of the second showing, five South Korean veterans in their eighties, four two-star generals, and an admiral, came on the stage to congratulate me for a great job. The audience applauded, and some had come onto the stage to congratulate me and express their appreciation for the film. The festival organizer set up a podium outside the theater, where viewers could have their photos taken with me.

I felt like I was at the Academy Awards.

CHAPTER FIFTY-TWO

Worldwide Honors

The Other Side of the Mountain began a tour of the world, and with it came more acclaim and recognition.

Chicago will always be special, a second home to us no matter where we were living. It was the city where I had met and married Kyuhee, the love of my life, where I had started my first job, and where our son Stephen was born. There was not a more apt place to have a second American film showing than at Chicago's Peace on Earth Festival.

It was emotional.

Among the more than 250 people attending were many Korean Americans, including old friends and family members. Once again, I was torn between the delight of having my friends see the result of my years of hard work—a side of me few people had known about—and the deep sadness of not having Kyuhee beside me to share the joy. Her absence in the city that meant so much to both of us made me deeply sad.

My interviews with Chicago area newspapers brought out the television and radio reporters for live interview at the theater entrance.

The festival was a success.

After the screening, the audience remained in their seats and stayed to engage in what became an hour-long question and answer session. There was no shortage of questions, and I answered them all.

"What inspired you to make the movie?"

"How difficult was it to shoot the film under unknown circumstances?"

"Were there any issues with the government?"

"What was the cost of making the movie?"

"How much of the story came from your own experiences?"

"What was your fondest memory of making the movie?"

The icing on the cake came when *The Other Side of the Mountain* was awarded Best Feature Film. It would be the first of many awards. The Chicago acclaim was followed by Best Feature Film and Special Jury Award at the Indonesia International Film Festival for Peace, Inspiration, and Equality in Jakarta, which I could not attend.

∽

An unexpected reward for *The Other Side of the Mountain* came from Yanji, China.

The Korean Chinese Art and TV Association asked me to show the film to the citizens of Yanji and Tumen City. I happily accepted the invitation for a two-day screening at a new three-hundred-seat cinema.

Years before, from 1920 to 1935, under Japanese occupation, many Koreans were forcibly resettled in cities and towns in Yanbian province. Their one million descendants now account for 43 percent of the 2.3 million residents.

I thought about people who had helped me build my factory in this region in Tumen City in 1997 to produce agricultural films for North Korean farmers. These were the same people who had devoted their time to helping me aid needy North Korean children. These included high-ranking civic officials, factory workers, and many Korean-Chinese citizens.

Official Chinese and Western sources estimate that about 400,000 Chinese soldiers (People's Volunteer Army) were either killed in action or died of disease, starvation, or exposure during the Korean War. Around 486,000 were wounded, out of around 3 million military personnel deployed in the war by China.

The Korean War left the mothers and grandmothers of the region heartbroken over the loss of their sons. Survivors, now elderly, told me the war left towns with no man strong enough to lift even a shovel.

I am enduringly fond of these calm and caring Korean-Chinese who live in such a cold, mountainous land. They teach their children the Korean native language and celebrate traditional Korean holidays wearing traditional Korean (hanbok) dresses. They treasure their ethnicity more than any group of Koreans I know anywhere in the world.

Many left the theater after the showing, sobbing and squeezing damp handkerchiefs. Most were elderly with small features, wrinkled faces, and shy smiles. They approached me and extended tiny but warm hands, just to touch me and say, "Thank you."

They are the purest, honest, warmhearted people I have known.

∽

The festival in San Francisco, so close to home, was special. Kyuhee was able to attend, to my delight, which meant the world to me. And many of my relatives, friends, and church folks were there to view the film enthusiastically.

As I introduced the film, I spoke about the night one young North Korean actress at the top of September Mountain, under a brilliant star-filled night sky, asked me if our film would be shown to the people in America. "I will show the film to the people in America," I promised her.

At that moment, I thought I heard someone from the crowded theater call out, "Grandpa, comrade, we are happy that you are showing the film to Americans." I looked for the pretty face in the dark theater, but I could not spot her; it was just my imagination. I wished she were there.

As I returned to my seat, my son Stephen held my hand as if to say, "Dad, you met your promise, congratulations."

Friends spoke in awe to me after the showing. "Joon, now we know where you have been hiding last five years. You have made this great movie."

∽

The New York Korean American Film Festival at a Manhattan theater was filled with second- and third-generation young Korean-Americans, which pleased me greatly. So many were sophisticated and educated. They seemed surprised at the depth and power of *The Other Side of the Mountain*. They were particularly interested in the film's story from a historical perspective, especially the Korean War.

During the question and answer session following the showing, a couple of the young students asked me about the No Gun Ri incident. A political science professor from nearby New York University, among the crowd, stood and told the questioner that every detail of the incident, as shown in the film, was historically accurate.

After a whirlwind of more successful showings, including the Lucerne International Film Festival in Switzerland, the New Jersey Film Festival, and seven others, I prepared for what I felt were two of the most important showings, for they would be in front of an audience directly affected by the message of *The Other Side of the Mountain*.

I was ready for South Korea.

CHAPTER FIFTY-THREE

Premiere in South Korea

South Korean law banned films made by North Koreans from being shown anywhere in the country. I was not deterred. My persistence and a bit of electoral luck finally paid off.

I had written to the Unification Ministry in Seoul in 2014 requesting permission for a showing. Unfortunately, the Ministry turned down my request that year and the following two years.

The Ministry's director gave me some small ray of hope when he told me that if Moon Jae In, one of three presidential candidates in 2017, who had campaigned on a more favorable relationship between South and North, won, then I might stand a chance.

Moon was elected as the president of South Korea that year and remains president today. That paved the way for *The Other Side of the Mountain*'s appearance at two South Korean film festivals.

In early 2018, I wrote President Moon. I told him of my twenty years of humanitarian aid to North Korea and my purpose in making the movie in the North—to tell our Korean sisters and brothers on both sides of the border to unite for peace and prosperity in the entire Korean peninsula. I enclosed a DVD of *The Other Side of the Mountain* with the letter.

Two weeks later, I received an email from the Blue House, the White House of South Korea, instructing me to contact the Ulsan Film Festival in Korea's southernmost province.

The premiere of *The Other Side of the Mountain* in the fall of 2018 was markedly significant, the first showing of a film to South Koreans made exclusively by North Koreans. It proved a great success, with leaders of both countries praising the moment as "a historically memorable accomplishment."

Once again, Kyuhee was unable to accompany me to Ulsan. At our front door in Pleasanton, leaving for Ulsan, I held her hands and kissed her goodbye. I told her I would return from the festival in a few days. Even with the growing sadness of the decline in her health, unable to stand from her wheelchair, Kyuhee looked at me and smiled.

"You are following your dream," she said. "I am so proud of you. Please do not be concerned about me. Please, deliver our messages at the festival, and come back to me safe."

I knew Kyuhee would want nothing less.

My younger brother Ken and his wife stayed with Kyuhee, as well as nurses and therapists who would attend to her every day while I was away. On the long trip to Ulsan, on the plane, in airport lounges, and during my overnight stay at a hotel—the entire time I was in Ulsan—I worried about Kyuhee's health. I missed her very much.

More than four hundred people filled every seat in the theater for two showings at the Ulsan Film Festival. At the conclusion of the first showing, the provincial governor walked onstage and awarded me with a trophy honoring my participation in the festival and my work toward a clearer understanding of the people and their situation in the North.

The usual question and answer session followed each showing. I was curious beforehand about the questions the South Korean audience would ask. To my surprise, no one asked if I had wanted *The Other Side of the Mountain* to promote communist ideology. One questioner asked how I chose the title of the film.

I told him.

"Before the turn of the century, common people did not have the means to travel over the mountains to visit the people on the other side. So, they always wondered about the people living there.

"Only if there were no mountains, people on both sides would have met and learned that there was no reason to fear one another—they would have seen that they were from the same stock and had the same interest in the pursuit of common human happiness."

There were other questions as well, and all pointed to a general concern.

"Do North Koreans want unification?"

"What do North Koreans think of South Koreans?"

"What was the situation regarding food shortages while you were in the North?"

"Is it true that Pyongyang makes the best-tasting naengmyeon?"

One older man stood up and shouted in a loud voice, "Why don't the big countries leave us alone and let us figure out our destiny between ourselves?"

An elderly lady asked me if there were any memorable stories I would like to tell. I recalled an appropriate story. I told her the Gomi story.

The hunter Song's dog Gomi, who I had named after my childhood German shepherd and protector at Wonsan apple farm, plays an essential role in the movie. I found a tiny white puppy running around the set and I asked Jang what the puppy was doing there. Jang told me that the order to cast the puppy came from the top.

The dog was a grandson of a puppy South Korean President Kim Dae-Joon gave to the Great Leader Kim Jung Il as a gift at the 2000 summit in Pyongyang. The Ministry thought that because *The Other Side of the Mountain's* theme was to promote unification, the third-generation puppy, the gift of the South Korean president, would be the right choice. I insisted Jang replace the puppy at all costs. He got a new hunting dog, Gomi, a big, brown, and furry, perfect for the part.

When I finished the story, they all laughed, laughed again, louder, and then the lady called out again, "You should have cast the puppy. We would be unified now."

I thought viewers were sensitive and fully understood the messages the movie delivered—that they were no different from their brothers and sisters in the North. Many commented that they understood the message of the love story of two young people, set in a beautiful landscape, and the North Korean people's hope for unification.

President Moon wrote me a letter expressing his admiration for my effort in aiding North Korea when its people were in desperate need of food. He appreciated my contribution toward the unification of the two Koreas through the movie, he said.

"The screening of *The Other Side of the Mountain* became an extraordinary opportunity to see the lives of our North Korean compatriots along with the scenic landscape. I believe having more of these cultural exchanges may bring the hearts of the South and North closer together. I hope that you will continue to work toward bringing peace and prosperity to the Korean Peninsula."

CHAPTER FIFTY-FOUR

Haeryong School

Severe floods in North Ham Kyung Book-Do province swept many towns into the Tumen River, which borders China, in 2016 and 2017. The worst destructive flood in 2016 destroyed many homes and schools leaving children without classrooms.

"The floods came through with such force, and they destroyed everything in their path. In Haeryong City, there was barely a building left unscathed," a Red Cross report noted. Hundreds died, and tens of thousands of people were displaced. The flooding destroyed essential crops, which in turn amplified existing and chronic food shortages.

The floods also created a later and tragic public health crisis.

I had been unable to visit North Korea since the beginning of 2013 because of my need to stay close to home and care for Kyuhee. A travel ban for US citizens was also put in place in 2017. Those impediments did not stop me from building a new school in Haeryong, a project I supervised from home.

As I expected, it become a big project. We began in spring 2017 and finished in fall 2018. I have yet to visit the school, but I am happy to say we built a strong and sturdy school building, and it has withstood the ravages of the constant floods since.

I put together a team for the project and asked Ms. Ahn to visit Haeryong to discuss with city managers the size of the building, its design, and materials we would need. I insisted the building be constructed with high-quality material, specifying heavy steel beams, a high-grade cement, fine wood doors and windows, thick tile roofs, hardwood floors, and heavy-duty large boilers to provide steady and reliable heat for the area's frigid and long winters.

Citizens joined to lay the school's foundations and erect its walls. Local carpenters framed the building and constructed desks and chairs.

It took two years to complete a three-story building that would accommodate 850 students and be sturdy enough to withstand future flooding. Everyone in Haeryong told Ms. Ahn, who visited the school from the start to the end of construction, that it is a beautiful school painted with vibrant yellow and orange colors.

I emphasized to the city administrators that the school is a gift from my mother.

Building a church was impossible in North Korea, but I succeeded in building a school and carried out her wishes. I felt relieved to know that the building would withstand the devastating storm, and the children would be in warm classrooms. It was named the Lee Yun Hee school in my mother's memory.

I recalled the story of King David my mother had told me during our long trek south to Busan. She told me God loved King David for his ultimate faith, his prayers for the forgiveness of his sins, and his love for his people. It was a story she intended to teach me Christian values. She often said, "Be humble, obey, and love God with all your heart and mind."

Kyuhee had done the same.

One New Year's Eve, in Sicily, in the small town of Agrigento, she and I walked down through the Valley of Temples. As we stopped at the first, Temple of Concordia, Kyuhee told me the stories of Abraham and Sarah. At the next temple she recounted the story of Isaac and Rebecca. At the third, I heard of Jacob and Rachel. When we reached the last temple, Tempio di Zeus, she told the story of Jesus. I was intrigued by Kyuhee's tales that night as she introduced me to the Bible in her lovely way.

My mother and Kyuhee planted the seeds of Christianity into my heart. Mother taught me the meaning of love, and Kyuhee demonstrated how to exercise it every day.

My mother would say to me, "I want you to go to your hometown, Haeryong, and build a Christian school someday. I want you to go there and help all the poor children." I *promised* my mother I would build the school.

Kyuhee was always supportive of my work and mission. She never shied from sacrifice and encouragement as she stood by my side.

Two ladies, my mother and Kyuhee, made me who I am and what I am.

CHAPTER FIFTY-FIVE

Caring for Kyuhee

On New Year's Day, 1996, when Kyuhee and I were staying at a small hotel in Erice, Sicily, at an elevation of 2,700 feet, she told me she felt a pain in her heart.

The small hotel had six rooms. Only one other room was occupied. The hotel staff was off for the holiday, leaving no one at the front desk. As soon as we checked into our room, Kyuhee felt the pain in her chest.

I called the hotel operator as her pain persisted, but no one answered. I tried to call my tour operator in Palermo, but they, too, had left for the holiday. I thought of taking her to Marsala, a nearby city, where I might be able to find a hospital.

At that moment, I thought about the time I was leaving Haeryong when our car was stranded on the snowbound mountain. I had prayed fervently to God to bring sunshine to melt the snow on the mountain road. That day God had answered my prayers.

I knelt by Kyuhee's bedside, placed my hands on her heart, and prayed to God to save my Kyuhee. An hour later, she felt no pain.

I knew that Kyuhee had a weak heart valve, mitral valve stenosis—sometimes called mitral stenosis—a narrowing of the heart's mitral valve. It is a condition prevalent in Asian women born in the 1900s who had suffered childhood pneumonia.

Dr. Alan Yeung, a Stanford University Hospital cardiologist, operated on her mitral valve in 1988, a year after the FDA approved the procedure. We visited Stanford hospital across the bay for regular checkups for the ten years we lived in Danville.

There were many nights when I had to take her to the emergency room because of sudden recurring heart pain.

I would have to admit her to a hospital many times, where she would stay for several days.

She had a cardioversion procedure to treat atrial fibrillation three times. Each time they poked Kyuhee's thin arm, hospital nurses had difficulty finding a vein for a blood sample. I wanted to be the one to feel the pain, not my Kyuhee.

Because of the long drive to Stanford from our house, Dr. Yeung suggested that we see his former student, Dr. Ramford Ng, who practices at Stanford Valley Care Health System in Pleasanton. He is a brilliant young cardiologist, and he took care of Kyuhee for years.

Each time Kyuhee was admitted to the hospital for a prolonged stay, I slept in her hospital room and comforted her around the clock. I would tell her stories of our many trips together and the fun we shared. One night I recalled an adventure in Sicily.

Driving from Palermo to Taormina, we stopped at the Shell station near Siracusa. The attendant filled the tank, and we paid for the gas. We left the gas station and drove about half an hour when Kyuhee noticed the gas gauge showed half-full. We looked at each other and said, "Yes."

We turned around, got lost on the way, and finally arrived back at the station. I drove the car right up to the pump, pulled out the nozzle, and filled the tank.

The attendant came out, shocked to see me. As I handed over the nozzle, after filling the tank full, I told him to his face, "Signore, do not cheat your overseas visitors again."

The man was yelling in Italian at us as we leisurely drove away. We were jubilant. On the two-hour drive to Taormina, we high fived with great enthusiasm time and time again.

I suppose he could have come out and ended the dispute with a shotgun. We were in Sicily, Mafia country, after all.

Any ordinary woman would have said, "Let's just forget this and not go back to the gas station and just go to Taormina before sunset."

No. Not Kyuhee.

✍

For our retirement we constructed a new house in Pleasanton in 2002. It was built to my exterior specifications, in the manner of a chateau in Southern France. Kyuhee took charge of the interior designs and color choices. Everyone says it is a beautiful house, with a fountain in a large pool to greet us and visitors.

✍

One morning, Kyuhee claimed she could not find the ring I had given her for her sixtieth birthday. She told me she suspected a cabinet installer had stolen it. I searched everywhere for two days and found it in a pocket of her old pajamas she seldom wore.

I wanted to understand more about the peculiar behaviors of a person at an early stage of memory loss. I began to learn as much as I could about the early symptoms of dementia. A medical journal article noted that suspecting or accusing others of stealing is one of the early symptoms of what would be a slow but chillingly irreversible decline.

Two years later, Kyuhee claimed that she could not find her driver's license. Again, I searched everywhere in the house but could not find it.

A driver's license represents much more than one would think. It is a pass, in a way, to freedom and independence. At her age, Kyuhee would be required to take a written examination to be issued a new license. We decided she would take it.

For five weeks, every morning after breakfast, we studied, together, poring over a test booklet of sample questions issued by the California

Department of Motor Vehicles. The written test to renew a license contains twenty-one questions; a passing score is at least eighteen correct answers. The questions on the test are in multiple-choice format and cover information about California signs and traffic laws.

One sample question dealt with the blood-alcohol threshold to be arrested for Driving Under the Influence (DUI), which is 0.08 percent. I knew that question would be on the exam.

I asked Kyuhee that question every morning. As confident as we could be, we went to the local DMV and waited two hours for the exam. Kyuhee headed into the private test area. I waited nervously outside, watching her, pen in hand, sit for the exam.

After what seemed like an hour, I could not bear to see her pondering the paper in front of her.

"It should not be taking this long," I thought. I walked into the exam room to offer some encouragement. I did not get far.

The exam administrator, a heavyset woman, watched me entering the restricted test area and shouted, loudly, "Mister, you can't be in the test area." I was embarrassed and quickly withdrew.

Kyuhee missed by a hair, by one question, four out of 21, but nonetheless did not pass.

Kyuhee missed the DUI question that we had emphasized repeatedly. Outside the exam room, we talked briefly about giving up, thinking she would most likely not drive much longer anyway. Her ID card would be enough for traveling, we reasoned.

That sentiment passed quickly. We both felt that we had failed and had lost part of our ability to participate fully in society.

The DMV allowed three consecutive exams on the same day. We looked at each other and said, "Yes. Let us do it again." After waiting two hours in line, Kyuhee took a second exam.

Again, she labored over the questions, and again I went into the room to encourage her, with the same result. "Sir, I told you not to go to the test area," the loud supervisor shouted.

Kyuhee passed. We were excited and relieved, but only for a moment.

My bane, the exam supervisor, walked over to us as we celebrated and told Kyuhee she had to answer three additional questions as a penalty for me being in the restricted area.

Kyuhee returned to the test area. I remained outside, prudently. She answered all three additional questions correctly.

As we walked out of the DMV building, we high fived and shouted with joy, "We did it. We did it," feeling as if we had successfully climbed Kilimanjaro.

I knew Kyuhee endured everything, the hours of study, the nervousness of sitting for the exam, the frustration of struggling for the answers, for me. I knew she had wanted to show me she was a capable and dependable wife. She wanted to show her appreciation for my effort to get her to pass the test. She wanted me to be proud of her. She did not want to fail.

I also know, deep inside, that her failing the DUI question on both tests, despite my repeated questioning during months of practice, indicated clearly that she was losing her memory. The brilliant woman who solved complicated Sudoku puzzles quickly and easily would have walked from the DMV exam room in just a few minutes with a perfect score.

There were other signs.

She began to develop an itchy and bloody scalp. I took her to a dermatologist who gave her medication and a special shampoo. Later, I learned she had not been massaging the shampoo into her scalp, only rinsing her hair when she showered. Once I started to wash her hair, scrubbing her scalp deeply, the itchiness disappeared.

Her neurologist continued to monitor Kyuhee's behavior and to prescribe new medications. None had any positive effect on her decline.

Dementia continued to steal her memory. I often took her to a favorite local park, pushing her in a wheelchair after wrapping a scarf carefully and gently around her neck and tucking a blanket over her legs. We would stop near a beautiful bonsai tree. I'd recount stories of our many happy travels. Kyuhee and I never dropped anchor.

We continued to move throughout our many years together, holding on to the faith, hope, and love we had for each other.

She was my love, my very existence.

To be with her and care for her, I sold my US company in 2013 to my respected competitor, Pactiv Corporation, in Deerfield, Illinois.

Promises

Helplessly watching Kyuhee's decline and her dramatically changing behavior, I was deeply saddened but resolved.

My endearing love for her strengthened my will to help her retain her dignity and live her life fully. As her dementia worsened, Kyuhee began to lose her trademark vitality and joy for life, but she still tried to hold on to her humor and pleasant demeanor.

Kyuhee always complimented others, praising everyone she met. "How pretty you are," she would tell strangers. "How handsome you are!"

Many days she spent in hospitals and nursing homes, eating bland institutional food while nurses and doctors took blood samples, gave her antibiotic injections, and made midnight changes of her underclothing had become regular. She was unable to see her grandsons, who were a refreshing light in her life.

She never complained. She always smiled at me and never refused the foods I had to hand-feed her. She allowed me to brush her teeth and help her shower without objection.

I arranged for physical, occupational, and speech therapists, who would come to our home every day to teach her how to chew, handle her hygiene, and help her maintain her ability to manage her life in her own small ways.

Every morning, Kyuhee, already awake, would greet me with a smile and clear eyes. I would open the drapes and raise her reclining bed. Then I would play a CD of a chorus singing hymns as sunlight and joyous music filled our bedroom. I would dress her, wash her her face and hands, and pat her with facial cream.

For her breakfast, I prepared a hard-boiled egg, a strip of crispy bacon, wheat toast with marmalade, and a slice of watermelon. It was a joy to feed her, to watch her eat, and to tell her stories of our travels together.

I got a high-functioning wheelchair, more like a recliner, with a nice cushion. I bought a Shower Buddy, a specially designed chair to take her in and out of the shower.

Her inexorable decline continued.

Her short-term memory began to desert her. I noticed she did not recognize her visiting friends, though she acted as if she did. Later, she stopped speaking even with my prompting. I had her sisters, friends, and our pastor talk with her over the phone. She listened, eyes blinking as if she understood, but she could not respond.

At night, I put her in bed, changed her briefs, dressed her in pajamas, daubed her with ointment, and tucked her into bed. I told her stories of our travels to places she loved.

One night, I told her the story of our trip to Egypt.

"Do you remember when we arrived in Cairo and climbed the pyramids and rode camels at sunset? You picked a tall female named Rosy, and we rode together, holding our hands above us, linked in love as we circled the pyramids. Remember?

"Do you remember that evening we saw Verdi's opera, *Aida*, in front of the Pyramid of Giza? You said that the best part of our trip to Egypt was the relaxing felucca ride, sailing on the Nile drifting in the warm, summer night breeze. Remember?

"We held hands and gazed at the bright moon reflecting on the mirror-like surface of the Nile. We kissed. Remember?"

Finally, she closed her eyes and drifted off to sleep with the memory of our loving, indescribable felucca ride. The next morning, as Kyuhee opened her eyes, she looked into mine as if to say, "I thank you for giving me a wonderful life, Joon. I love you."

One night, I awoke and saw Kyuhee's mouth agape as she struggled to breathe. I had to accept the fact that she was getting worse.

I knelt by her bed and prayed to God. I asked God for another miracle, like the ones I received at the top of the snow-covered mountain in North Korea and in Sicily when her heart pain had persisted.

I called an ambulance.

She was admitted to the Stanford Valley Care Hospital and stayed for two days. The doctors and nurses did everything they could, taking a series of MRIs and X-rays.

At the end of the second day, the hospital could not feed her nor give her any medications. The doctor in charge told me she had fluid in her lungs. I sensed he was hoping I would take Kyuhee to an end-of-life hospice. I brought her home, instead, so I could care for her myself.

Our pastor's wife, who had some nursing experience, and a church friend who worked at hospice, stayed with us throughout the ensuing nights to help me.

As Kyuhee lay in bed, I held her hands for two days, listening to her breathing, administering oxygen, checking the pulse-oximeter, and watching her face.

I looked at her slightly opened mouth and heard her breathing.

The intervals between her breaths became longer. In her final moment, she stirred and looked into my eyes.

She was saying goodbye.
She stopped breathing.

I asked God for her to breathe one more time. At that moment, I became peaceful, seeing her leaving me for a place where she could breathe freely and wait for me to join her.

My dearest wife, Kyuhee, passed away
at 7:26 a.m. on October 26, 2019.

223

Looking at her peaceful face, I thanked God for keeping her so beautiful and graceful until the end.

The five years I cared for her were as happy as the times we traveled all over the world together.

In the early afternoon, both our sons came to their mother's bedside. I asked the pastor's wife if Kyuhee could remain one more day at home.

I held her hands all day and kept them from becoming cold.

As the time approached for the hearse from the funeral home to take her from me, my anxiety increased. My heart was shaking. I held her hands and prayed to God to stop time. I wished the hearse would have a flat tire.

The driver arrived with a gurney and placed Kyuhee in a body bag. As he was about to pull up its zipper, I asked him to leave the bag open so I could see Kyuhee's face for a second longer. I told him to drive very carefully.

When he pushed the gurney into the back compartment of the hearse, I asked him to remain in the driveway just for a few more seconds so I could see Kyuhee through the rear window.

It was the saddest moment in my life.

My son James held me as I clung to the hearse before it finally drove away. I sat, frozen, on the stone pavement until my sons brought me into the house.

The funeral service took place at the Oakmont Memorial chapel. Reverend Jason Jeon read Psalm 91:1-4 and 1 Corinthians 15:51-58 to our family and friends from Korea, China, and the States. My niece Susan from New Jersey, who Kyuhee loved dearly, and our grandson Ian delivered the eulogies.

"Auntie exemplified through her life the meaning of true Christianity," Susan told the gathering.

"My grandmother was a living embodiment of selfless devotion to others," Ian reflected.

Three months later, January 2020, I went to San Quintin, Mexico, a small town in Baja, California, near Ensenada. I wanted to explore how I could offer support to a Christian missionary group helping poor Indios who worked on local farms.

I stayed at the Mission Santa Maria Hotel, by the Bahia Santa Maria beach. In the early morning of the twenty-third, I walked the empty beach, watching the sun rise over the calm Gulf of California.

"Where are you, Kyuhee?" I shouted.

"Joon, I am right here.

Why are you shouting?"

I knew Kyuhee was there with me.
She is in my heart always, always, and forever.

∽

I took a sip of chardonnay on Valentine's Day, her birthday. I told her of my plans to write a book about our life together. I *promised* her I would continue to support the orphans, the farms, and the school, and that I would devote my remaining life to educating young people in both Koreas to pave the way to unify their homeland. I *promised* her one day we would again ride our camels holding our hands high as we circled the pyramid.

I kissed Kyuhee on the engraved picture on the head stone and walked slowly away. I stopped and glanced back at her one more time as tears creased my face.

I then turned toward my next adventure, always knowing, as in life, that Kyuhee is walking right beside me, looking at me with love.

Acknowledgments

I am deeply thankful to Tom McCarthy for his vital part in transforming my manuscript into this book. I'm grateful for his thoughtfulness and passion for the story.

I would like to express my appreciation to Leah Nicholson for loving my story and bringing it out into the world.

I am also thankful to Christella and Robert Brandes and Ken Bai, Jr. for their early review of the manuscript and helpful feedback.

To appreciate my story more fully, please, watch the videos and the movie.

Links to the video:

1. Memorial for Kyuhee
   https://vimeo.com/309993374
   Password: life

2. Documentary for North Korea aids
   https://vimeo.com/134323021
   Password: Love

To learn about the movie,
"The Other Side of the Mountain"
visit the website:

www.osomfilm.com

Biography of Joon Bai

1937: Born in Haeryong, Ham Kyung Book-Do, North Korea

1956: Graduated Kyunggi High School in Seoul, Korea

1957–1958: Served South Korean Military (ROK)

1966: Graduated University Missouri, School of Engineering (BSME)

1966–1972: Corporate Quality Control Manager: Extrudo Film Corporation, Lake Zurich, IL

1973–1978: Regional Sales Manager: Northern Petrochemical Company, Jolliet, IL

1979: Founder—V.P. General Manager: North American Film of California, Tustin, CA

1983: Founder—CEO: Trans Western Polymers, Inc., Livermore, CA

1995: Chairman: Trans Western Polymers, Inc., Tamaqua, PA

1997: Founder—Chairman: Trans Western Yanbian, Inc., Tumen City, Republic of China

2005–2012: Writer and Producer of feature film, *The Other Side of the Mountain*—Awarded recognitions from domestic and international film festivals

2013: Resigned from TWP, Tamaqua

2019: Resigned from TWP, Yanbian

2019–2022: Author of book, *Promises*

2013–2022: Author of book, "Where the Azalea Flowers Blossom." (available in Spring 2023)

.

Family photo: Mother, Joon, Ben, Father, Carl,
Nanny Hoeryong, North Korea, 1937

Front row: Chung Sook, Mother, Father, Ken
Back row: Carl, Ben, Joon
Busan, South Korea, 1954

Graduation, Kyunggi High School, 1957

Mother in Seoul, 1972

Graduation at Yonsei University, Seoul, 1957
Kyuhee, second row, 6th from left

Yonsei University Hospital, 1958
Kyuhee on the right

Somewhere between Pyongyang and Seoul, 1953

Train to Busan, 1953

Crossing a destroyed bridge
near Kaesong, 1953

Our wedding in Chicago, 1964

Graduation, University of Missouri, 1966

Student apartment
in Columbia, Missouri, 1965

Chicago apartment
in Rolling Meadows, 1966

Welcoming Mother to the United States, 1974

At Yosemite with Mother, 1975

James and Steve with Fuzzy and her four
puppies in Joliet, Illinois, 1975

My dear friend Song Suk Hwang at Pebble Beach, 1994

Choir members who traveled to Seoul for a choir competition, 1992
Kyuhee, second row, first from left

TWP Yanbian factory, 2000

TWP Yanbian factory, 2000   TWP Tamaqua factory, 1999

First vacation to San Francisco, 1972

Matterhorn in Switzerland, 1984

Schonbrunn Palace Garden, Vienna, 1986

London, 1986

Florence, 1988

Beijing, 1998

Jeju Island, 1999

Wedding anniversary in San Diego, 1989

London theater, 1990

Alaska, 1990

Kyoto, Japan, 1993

Egypt, 1999

Hong Kong, 1998

With Masai Mara Chiefs,
Kenya, 2000

Walking safari at Kruger National Park,
South Africa, 2005

Taj Mahal, 2003

Lake Louis, Canada, 2001

With Lenin and Nicholas II at Moscow, Russia, 2006

The Dead Sea, Lebanon, 2009

Petra, Jordan, 2009

London Olympics, 2012

James' graduation at Columbia University Graduate School, 1994

Steve's graduation at New York University, 1991

James in Pyongyang, North Korea, 1998

Steve in Kenya, 2000

Family at James' wedding, 2000

Four brothers at James' wedding
(left to right) Carl, Joon, Ben, and Ken

James and Stephan on James' wedding day, 2000

Steve's wedding, 2002

Family in Hawaii, 2005

Luke, Jonah, and Aaron, 2013

Ian's first birthday, 2005

Luke and Ian with local boys, Kenya, Africa, 2018

Tanzania, Africa, 2018

Grandson Jonah, Milan, Italy, 2019

Grandson Ian, Bodega Bay, California, 2019

25 pound salmon

Aaron and Jonah, Bodega Bay, 2021

Golden Gate Bridge, San Francisco, 2021

Ae Yko Won orphanage,
2–4 month old orphans
cared for by a nurse,
Chongjin, North Korea, 1997

Kyuhee and Joon visit
2–4 year old orphans,
Chongjin, North Korea, 1998

Caring for an orphan,
Chongjin, North Korea, 1998

Elementary school, Gilju, North Korea, 1999

Accordian concert at Chongjin Middle School, North Korea, 2005

Concert by Chongjin Middle School in honor of Joon Bai, North Korea, 2005

Corn Field in Heoryong, North Korea, 1997

Agricultural film,
Hamgyong, North Korea, 1998

Greenhouse in Hamgyong, North Korea, 1999

Farm Corporative Leaders, 1999

Greenhouse in Heoryong, North Korea, 2001

Snowbound, 2000

Bread factory, Puryong City, North Korea, 2005

Kim Il-Sung Plaza, Pyongyang,
North Korea, 2005

Director Jang, In Hak, Joon Bai,
Production Coordinator Rim, Myung Jin

Music Composer of the soundtrack,
Song, Dong Hwang

Director, 2008

Sun A in action, 2008

Shooting reunion scene, 2009

Singing of the Unification Song, 2012

Leading Actor, Kim, Ryung Min, Actress, Kim, Haen Sook
their Child Jin Hae

80th Birthday of Joon Bai and family reunion at Sonoma, 2017

Love

Niece Paula and Douglas, 2016

Middle-high school built after 2017 flood
Named after my mother
Haoryong, North Korea, 2019

Resting Place, Oakmont, California, 2021

Letter from President Moon Jae-in of South Korea, 2018

배병준 님께,

멀리 미국에서 보내주신 편지는
대통령님께 잘 전해드렸습니다.
따뜻한 성원에 깊이 감사드립니다.

"산 너머 마을"의 울주영화제 상영은
북녘의 산하와 함께
북녘 동포들의 삶을 볼 수 있는
매우 특별한 기회가 되었습니다.
이러한 문화교류가 많아질수록
남과 북의 마음도
더욱 가까워질 것이라고 생각합니다.

평화와 번영의 한반도로 가는 길에
앞으로도 계속
힘을 보태주실 것으로 믿습니다.

변함없는 성원 부탁드리며,
늘 건강하고 행복하시길 기원합니다.

대통령비서실 드림

Dear Mr. Byung Joon Bai

The Screening of *The Other Side of the Mountain* became an extraordinary opportunity to see the lives of our North Korean compatriots along with the landscape of land.

I believe having more of these cultural exchanges may bring the hearts of the South and North closer together.

I hope that you will continue to work toward bringing peace and prosperity to Korean Peninsula.

I wish you the good health and happiness.

Moon Jae-in
President of Korea